Foster Parenting

The Ballard Family
Brock & Julie
Courtney, Lyric & Lexi
1927 Green Meadow Drive
Jefferson City, MO 65101

Foster Parenting

A Simple Guide to Understanding What It's All About

Stacie Craig

Starik Publishing

Slaton, Texas

A Division of Starik Inc.
www.starikpublishing.com

Cover and interior design by Erik Craig, Starik Publishing

Copyright © 2007 by Stacie Craig

All rights reserved. No part of this publication may be reproduced, stored in a retrieval system or transmitted in any form or by any means, electronic, mechanical, photocopying, recording, or otherwise without the prior written permission of the copyright holder, except brief quotations used in a review.

Notice: This book is designed to provide information on all aspects of foster care. It is sold with the understanding that the publisher and author are not engaged in rendering legal, accounting or other professional services. Such topics, as discussed herein, are for example or illustrative purposes only. If you need legal, financial, or other professional assistance, you should use the services of an appropriately qualified professional where you can explore the unique aspects of your situation and can receive specific advice tailored to your circumstances.

The purpose of this guide is to educate and entertain. The author and Starik Publishing shall have neither liability nor responsibility to any person or entity with respect to any loss or damage caused, or alleged to have been caused, directly or indirectly, by the information in this book.

If you do not wish to be bound by the above, you may return this book to the place where purchased or the publisher for a full refund.

Library of Congress Control Number: 2007905555
ISBN 978-1-934684-00-9

Published by
Starik Publishing
P.O. Box 307
Slaton, Texas 79364

Printed in the United States of America

ACKNOWLEDGMENTS

This book would not have been possible if not for the encouragement and assistance of my husband, Erik. I would like to thank Glynna Strait, Ginger Summerlin, Carrie Dunn and all those who read the manuscript and offered valuable suggestions for its improvement. I especially thank Ann Bailey for providing me with information and answering all my questions. I am grateful to all the foster parents and caseworkers who answered my questions, and to all caseworkers, foster parents and concerned individuals who do their best to improve the lives of abused and neglected children everywhere.

To all the foster parents, past, present and future, who willingly give of their time and love to help children in need.

Table Of Contents

Introduction — How I Got Started
11
Chapter One — Why Choose to be a Foster Parent
13
Chapter Two — What To Do First
19
Chapter Three — Where Do The Children Come From
27
Chapter Four — When The Child Comes
31
Chapter Five — How Busy Will You Be
41
Chapter Six — What You Need To Know About Court
47
Chapter Seven — Who Is The Child's Best Advocate
53
Chapter Eight — When A Child Goes Home
57
Chapter Nine -- What Are The Greatest Challenges
63
Chapter Ten — What Are The Major Financial Concerns
73
Chapter Eleven — What Happens If You Are Investigated
79
Chapter Twelve — How Do You Adopt From The System
83
Chapter Thirteen — Who Else Will Be Involved
95
Chapter Fourteen — What Resources are Available
101

Table Of Contents

Chapter Fifteen — How Will It End
107
Aprendix A — Supply Checklist
111
Appendix B — Questions to Keep Near Your Phone
113
Appendix C — Abuse Hotlines and State Websites
115
Glossary of Terms and Acronyms
119

Introduction

How I Got Started

When my husband and I were first married, we discussed the possibility of adopting at some future date. Years later, we had a son, our first and only biological child. We wanted to adopt our next child, but could not afford a traditional adoption. We decided foster care was the right solution for us. We began our training process shortly after that. I became pregnant again during this time, but miscarried a few weeks later. We continued our certification process and were certified nearly one year after beginning the process.

We became certified as a foster/adopt home in February of 2004 and received our first placement about two weeks later. That child stayed only five days. Our next child came about two weeks after that, who became our first adoption. We added one more in July of that year, who became one of our last two adoptions. In April of the following year, we added a "legal risk" foster child, who became our second adoption. I'll explain "legal risk" in Chapter 12: How Do You Adopt from the System. Our fifth placement was in November of that year. This was also one of our last two adoptions who were adopted at the same time because they were natural siblings. Their adoption took place approximately one year following our second adoption.

We had several challenges during our time as foster parents and throughout the adoption process and begin seeking out anything that would help us overcome these challenges. What we discovered was that there was little information available on the subject of foster parenting. At that time, I decided to write a book on the subject so that others would have a reference to use that covered the basics of foster parenting. Throughout our time as foster parents, we encountered many unique experiences and many others common to most foster parents. Many of our experiences, as well as those of other foster parents, have gone into this book so that you will be prepared for whatever awaits you.

My hope, in writing this book, is to present new foster parents and those interested in foster parenting with a guide to help you with your journey. I have tried to make it simple enough for anyone to understand without compromising the usefulness of the information. You may want to read this book from beginning to end to gain an understanding of the entire process, or you may choose to only read those chapters of immediate concern to you. Whichever method you use, I hope you gain valuable incite from these words to aid you in your search for information.

After three years as foster parents, we now have five children: a biological son, an adopted son, and three adopted daughters. Five years separates our oldest child from our youngest, with three others in between. It took us approximately four years, including our training time, to get to this point. Most foster families do not keep this many of their placements, but we are proof that it is possible. Keep reading to find out what you need to do to foster or adopt children of your own.

Chapter One

Why Choose to be a Foster Parent

Going to college. Moving to a new town. Getting married. Having a baby. These are just some of the important decisions we make in our lives. The decision to become a foster parent is just as important. This decision will affect every aspect of your life and the lives of every other member of your family, from this point onward. This is not a decision to be taken lightly.

Foster care is considered by many as a "black sheep". It brings to mind pictures of hurting children and abusive parents. Many people believe that foster parents are lower class citizens because they take in "those children". Others believe that only the rich can be foster parents because it takes a lot of money to raise someone else's child. I want to dispel these myths. I agree that foster parenting is not for everyone, but it can be for you. To foster means to nurture and to care for something. This is not a negative word. Caring and nurturing children is what all parents should do. What sets foster parents apart from other parents is that foster children are not legally related to us. This simply means that the child was not born to or previously adopted by the foster parent. Being a foster parent is not the same as parenting your own children, but it should not be thought of as a job only for other people.

So, who can be a foster parent? The answer is actually quite broad. Foster parents can be young or old, single, married or widowed. They can be of any race or religion. A foster parent may have biological or adopted children at home or who have already left home, or they may not have any children at all. They can be rich or fairly poor. Any number of people can be foster parents, but there are some requirements.

Prospective foster parents must be at least 21 years of age, be willing to attend training, have adequate space, submit to a home study and be willing to care for children who have been abused or neglected. In addition to these requirements, you must have patience. The process of becoming a foster parent is lengthy and the delays can be frustrating, but the rewards are even greater.

Before you become a foster parent you need to think hard about why you want to be one. The reasons for being a foster parent vary greatly from one family to the next. When asked this question foster parents gave the following answers: "To help children who needed a home and a meal". "To adopt a child in need of a home". "To make a difference in a child's life". "To make a significant contribution to our society's future by positively impacting our children". "Because there is a need for foster parents". Other reasons included "wanting more children" or "playmates for our child". Some had been foster children themselves and wanted to give something back. Some just loved having children in their homes. Your answer may match one of these or you may have other reasons, but whatever your motivation, be sure you are aware of it.

The children would not be in care if they came from good, healthy families.

Before you decide, you should know that it is not easy. Being a foster parent is more than a full-time job. Unlike other jobs, there is no "quitting time." You cannot leave this job and take a vacation and you do not get weekends off. These are children who need your love, help and constant care. They come with problems and challenges unique to their individual situations and pasts. If you cannot give these children your full effort and time, you should not take this job. This does not mean that you have to give up everything, just that you cannot enter this job lightly.

If you decide you can handle these problems, you must next think of your family. Does your spouse, if you have one, also want to be a foster parent? Can they handle these children and their problems? It is very important that you and your spouse agree before the decision to foster is made. Your relationship must be strong enough to withstand the pressures foster parenting brings. Adding children to any family can cause strain on relationships, but foster children come with additional problems caused by their previous living situations. They also bring with them the added strain of caseworkers and paperwork. The children in foster care depend on your relationship being strong. Remember, they would not be in care if they came from good, healthy families.

You may also want to consider the opinions of your extended families and your friends. If you have a close relationship to your or your spouse's parents, how do they feel about foster care? Will they treat the foster children the same as their other grandchildren or will they have difficulty accepting them. Their attitudes toward foster care may affect your relationships with them. If there are any other relatives you are close to, you should consider their thoughts and opinions as well. The opinions of these other relatives will probably not be as important to your decision as those of your immediate family, but it is helpful to know how they feel. If anyone strongly disagrees with your decision, your relationship with that person will be affected.

This decision may also affect your relationships with your friends. It is nice to think that all your friends will be as happy with your decision as you are and support you 100 percent, but that is not always the case. Your relatives and friends may not understand why you want to be a foster parent. They usually want what is best for you and what will make you happy, but they may see only the negative aspects of fostering. You will have to help them understand your motivation, so again, it is better to be perfectly clear on your motivation. You may also need to educate them on the positive aspects of fostering to help them understand your motivation.

Foster children come with a lot of baggage including, but not limited to, sexual, physical and emotional abuse, neglect, medical problems, and malnutrition. Many do not know how to care for themselves. Many do not know how to clothe or bathe themselves, do not know basic hygiene, or even how to eat or feed themselves. There are many challenges to overcome. Many foster children come from homes where they were forced to parent themselves. They were never taught the basic skills necessary to function in society. They only learned what they could figure out for themselves, and what they teach themselves is often not appropriate or healthy.

One of my family's first placements was a nine month old baby. This baby did not know how to eat, and he was extremely thin. We spent two long days trying to get him to eat. He only drank one bottle for each of those days. We were very concerned about his health. With persistence, by the third day, we had him drinking and eating. He ate everything we could feed him for the next two weeks before settling into a normal, healthy eating pattern.

Foster Care is a decision that not only affects you but your children also.

We were lucky. This baby's problem was easily solved, but many are not. Each child is unique, as are their problems and histories. Some of these problems and challenges will be discussed later in the book, but you need to know that no matter how much you think you are prepared, there will always be surprises. Because of these extra challenges, this decision goes beyond deciding to have a child (which is also a decision not to be taken lightly).

If you have any biological children or previously adopted children, be sure to consult them before deciding to foster. Make sure your children understand what you are planning to do. Help them to understand on their level. If your children are very young, they will probably not understand until you bring another child home. Slightly older children can be told that "another child or baby is coming to live with us for awhile." If the child is old enough to understand, you should ask for their approval. Your children do not have to agree, but remember, this decision concerns them as much as you. They will be sacrificing a lot because of your decision. They will now be sharing their house, their toys and most importantly you. They may have added responsibility. Your children know your house rules and how to behave. They will therefore, have to model these behaviors and demonstrate the role of a child in a family. They also, need to know the children are being placed with you temporarily. They may leave your home at any time. Help your children to also see the positive side of fostering: they will have a new sibling and a constant playmate.

I have said all of this to help you understand the gravity of your decision of whether to foster or not. However, do not make that decision yet. There is much more to think about before you decide.

There are many benefits to foster parenting for yourself, your family and the children for whom you will provide care. There is a lot of satisfaction knowing that you provided or are providing for a child when they most need it. You are giving them a loving, caring, safe family, which many of these children have never had. Because of you, they are being fed throughout the day, every day. They have clean clothes to wear and they have discipline and structure. Most of all, they have love.

By caring for these children, you are giving their birth parents a chance to turn their lives around so that they can care for their children safely. Because you are providing a safe home for their child, the birth parents do not have to worry about their child while following their "plan of service." This gives them more time to focus on fixing the problems with their own lives while their child is learning to be a part of a functional family.

Watching the changes a child goes through is another rewarding aspect of foster parenting. Many children begin improving almost instantly. They thrive on the love, care, and guidance you give them and change dramatically. The situation the child came from and how long they lived in those conditions will determine how quickly these changes occur; but they will occur. It is very rewarding to watch a young child learn and grow. Our malnourished infant could barely crawl when he arrived at our house. In about a month, he was not only crawling, but walking. This same baby could barely eat, but in a short time he became a hearty eater and a very healthy young boy. Sometimes a child may be physically healthy, but not know how to smile or react to people. It is very rewarding to see a child such as this learn to smile and then laugh.

For those of you considering adoption, foster care is an excellent way to proceed. A child being adopted must be in your care, in the state of Texas, for six months before the adoption can proceed. This waiting period gives you the opportunity to get to know the child you are planning to adopt. During this time, you will learn what it is like to have a child in your home, what challenges they will create for you and your family, what new expenses you will have and how much time and energy they will require. The child will also learn what it is like to live in your family, what is expected of them, what they can expect from you. After this time is over, you and the child will know for sure whether the adoption is best for your family. Later in the book, I will give more details concerning adopting from the foster care system.

Chapter Two

What to do First

You have decided to become a foster parent, so now what? The first thing you should do is make a phone call. You need to contact your local Department of Family and Protective Services (DFPS). Many states use other names for this department such as the Department of Children and Family services or the Department of Human Services. A list of each state and its official website has been provided in the appendix. You can also find the telephone numbers for your local department by searching under state departments for human services. For simplicity, I will refer to this department as the Department of Family and Protective Services, DFPS or Child Protective Services, CPS. Inform the receptionist that you are interested in becoming a foster parent. They should be able to connect you with the appropriate person. With the potential privatization of foster care, you may need to contact a private agency instead of DFPS. If this is the case, DFPS should be able to provide you with a list of agencies in your area.

You may be asked for your name and address, and will either be sent information or will be asked to attend an orientation meeting. This meeting is designed to inform you about fostering and to begin the necessary paperwork. You will be given very basic information at this time. This is not a training meeting and you will not learn much about foster parenting at this time. It is only to separate those who are not going to put forth the necessary effort to become a foster parent from those who might.

The next step is training. The state uses a Parent Resource for Information Development Education (PRIDE) training program. Some private agencies also use this training method, but many adopt their own systems. The training phase generally consists of eight to ten weeks of classes one night each week, and you will have approximately 40 hours of training during this time. If you are married, your spouse will also be required to attend this training.

These classes are designed to prepare you for foster parenting, although many foster parents do not believe they are effective or adequate. Some feel the information presented does not portray the realities of foster parenting. Much of the material is outdated and does not focus on today's issues. There are many scenarios presented during this training that seem to gloss over the true challenges foster parenting presents. I am not saying this training is useless. On the contrary, it does begin to illustrate and open your mind to what you can expect later. What it does not do, is give enough detail about the challenges you will face or present enough solutions to these challenges.

Once you have completed the training and still desire to be a foster parent, the rest of the certification process begins. During this process, you will submit to a home study which is an extended interview process in which your life is closely examined. It consists of several visits to your home. You will be required to fill out paperwork and forms concerning nearly every aspect of your life. These forms request basic identifying information including name, age, height, hair color and eye color for each family member. They also require you to list every residence you have had over the last ten years, personal references, income and expenses, health coverage, activities you engage in, your hobbies and any other information that might assist in determining if you are a suitable household for caring for children. Your references will be checked and your parents and your spouse's parents will be contacted as well. They are asked questions concerning your ability to foster and your strengths and weaknesses.

Every member of your family will be interviewed together and individually. This interview includes all children and adults living in your house. As strange as it may seem, even very young children are interviewed at this time. There is also a home check to make sure your house meets the minimum standards required by law for child care. A copy of the areas to be checked can be provided to you prior to this check so that you may prepare.

There are many restrictions placed on foster parents concerning their homes that will be checked during the home check. Some of the restrictions that are most difficult to follow are those concerning firearms, trampolines and swimming pools. Firearms and their ammunition must be locked up separately. In fact, firearms, hunting knives, bows and arrows, and any other weapons must be locked up. Trampolines, some jungle gyms, and some swinging equipment are also forbidden. Swimming pools also carry heavy restrictions. They must have covers or be surrounded by a high fence with a locked gate. When in use, there must be a water safety certified adult supervising the children at all times. These are just a few of the restrictions placed on these and other items you may have. For a complete list, read the minimum standards for your state.

Each member of your household will be tested for Tuberculosis (TB), including your children. This is a simple test in which an injection is given to you in your forearm, just under the skin. In a couple of days, it is checked by your doctor for any reaction. You and your spouse must also complete Cardio Pulmonary Resuscitation (CPR) and first aid classes. The primary caregiver is required to maintain their certification for as long as you remain a foster parent. This means you must attend a refresher course in CPR every year (two years in some places) and renew your first aid certification every three years. The American Red Cross, colleges and universities and some medical offices can assist you with this certification.

A criminal history check is conducted on every adult member of your household. Anyone living in your house who is 18 years of age or older is considered to be an adult. Most states also require you to be fingerprinted, especially if you have recently moved from another state. All pets must have current rabies vaccinations. If you are a smoker, you will be required to not smoke in your house for the safety of the foster children.

You will also need to have a fire inspection of your home. This is a checklist of fire hazards that may be present. For example, all foster homes are required to have a fire extinguisher, smoke detectors and in many cases, carbon monoxide detectors. A home health check must also be completed. It is another checklist used for identifying potential health and safety risks. The questions on this list concern items such as general cleanliness of your home and yard, and whether adequate water is available. A complete copy of the checklist for either of these inspections can be obtained at your local DFPS. Your region may require additional tests or inspections before you can be certified.

> *Certification status can be checked at any time by contacting the worker assigned to your case.*

There are few costs involved with the certification process. You will be expected to pay for the TB tests and for your CPR and first aid training, but all other requirements are generally free. After all of the training, testing, inspecting and interviewing is completed, a report must be completed by the home study specialist. This may take a few weeks or months depending on the caseload of this worker. During this time, there is little you can do but wait. If you move, have a child or any other major life changes occur during this time, the home study must be updated and in some cases redone. After it is completed it must be updated periodically and especially any time a major change occurs.

My family's certification process took almost exactly one year from the orientation meeting until the certificate arrived. This delay was in part due to a move from one region to another during the home study phase. It is possible for this process to be shorter or much longer depending on caseload and your particular circumstances. Try to be patient during this time, but remember, you can check on the status of your certification process at any time by contacting the worker assigned to your case.

Now is the time to locate a good attorney. There are times, as a foster parent, when you may need their services. You may need them to assist in progressing a child's case, for the adoption of a foster child and for representing you through an investigation. Finding one at this stage in the certification process will allow you immediate access to assistance when the need arises. The importance of having an attorney and how to locate a good one are discussed throughout this book.

During this certification time you must decide what kind of foster home you will be. This can be a group or single family home, basic care or therapeutic. A foster group home requires a more structured environment than a single family home. You can be certified to take in 7 to 12 children at a time as opposed to a maximum of six in a foster family home. The requirements for room sizes and living areas differ as well, requiring greater available floor space for each child. A group home also requires a more structured daily schedule and stricter guidelines for daily life. The entire list of guidelines for all types of foster homes can be found in the minimum standards.

Another decision will be what level of care you will provide. A "basic care" home provides care for children who require basic services. These children are usually fairly normal for their age level. They may have mild developmental delays, mild behavioral problems, and may require some special medical care. Most of the problems you will encounter with these children can be overcome with time and proper guidance.

A "therapeutic home" may care for basic needs children, but they may also care for therapeutic children. Private agencies require all their foster parents to be certified as therapeutic regardless of the type of child they will care for. Therapeutic children may include children who require more structure and more constant supervision. These children may have some physical aggression, some behaviors that are harmful to themselves or to others or moderate medical conditions requiring special care. They may exhibit any or all of these conditions. Other problems such as drug abuse may also exist. A therapeutic home may care for children who exhibit a lot of self-injurious actions or are medically fragile. These children require more constant supervision and monitoring. Some of these children may attempt suicide or try to burn down your house. They require extra attention and love and it takes a special foster parent to handle challenges of this nature.

When a child enters foster care, the state ascertains what level of care a foster child requires. The child is then labeled as level one, two, three, four or five. Basic care is for levels one and two. Level two children may also be considered therapeutic as are levels three and four. Level five is reserved for children who require constant care and supervision and may be institutionalized. One foster mom I surveyed had children who were basic as well as therapeutic children. She stated that the basic leveled children may have had the same challenging behavioral issues as the therapeutic children. The only difference was that the basic child was not on medication. The state requires documented proof that a child has a serious problem before they will level them therapeutic. If you believe you have a child who is incorrectly leveled, you will need to get a medical opinion in writing before they can be re-leveled. The state is a government agency and will often try to level a child as low as they can to save money. You may have to fight to have them re-leveled.

Whichever type of foster home you decide to become certified as, your decision is not set in stone.

It is also possible to be certified as a Primary Medical Needs (PMN) home. This designation is for a foster home that cares for children who are medically fragile. They may have medical conditions that require the use of feeding tubes or other medical apparatus. They may only be able to provide a minimum level of care for themselves. Many of these homes care for only infants. It is also not uncommon to have one of these medically fragile children die while in your care. Special training is essential to care for these children and not all foster parents are mentally and physically equipped to provide care for them.

Children with extremely severe problems may be institutionalized if the need exists, but many are placed in homes. This is another level of care that you may provide. Many foster parents specialize in this type of care. They may keep only medically fragile children, who are considered to be PMN children. These children have extensive medical needs and require full-time supervision and care. They may require additional monitoring systems and a greater medical knowledge. These children will require more time and attention than a basic or possibly even a therapeutic child will require.

As you can see, there are many possible levels of care you can provide. Foster parents are needed for each of these levels of care. The higher therapeutic levels of care require more annual training. You must receive specialized instruction in the care of special needs children. There is a minimum of 30 hours training required per caregiver, with a 50 hour minimum per home. In other words, if you are a single parent home, you will be required to fulfill all 50 hours of training yourself.

Whichever type of foster home you decide to become certified as, remember, your decision is not set in stone. If you are certified for children ages 0-17 and later decide you would prefer only infants, you can change your certification or just refuse to accept older children. If you are certified for therapeutic and decide you would rather be certified for primary medical needs, you can receive the proper training and change your certification. My family was initially certified for two children, but that number was changed every time we adopted a child or decided to take one more. One foster mother surveyed said "we were only going to foster one or two." She said that in 24 years she had taken in more than 150 children. Other foster parents claimed to have fostered 250, 350 and for one family 477 children! Of course, you never have to change your mind and it is perfectly acceptable to foster only one or two children. In my case we continued adding children until we had reached the state's limit. I agree completely with the advice of one foster mother who said, "Enjoy yourself, it's very addicting."

Chapter Three

Where do the Children Come From

Child Protective Services (CPS) is a division of the Department of Family Protective Services (DFPS). CPS is charged with investigating all allegations of child abuse or neglect. These allegations are made by concerned individuals by way of state hotlines, teachers, day care providers, medical personnel and others who come in contact with the child(ren). The national hotline abuse number is 1-800-4-A-Child or 1-800-252-2873. The Texas hotline number is 1-800-252-5400, or a report can be made at www.txabusehotline.org. Other state hotlines are listed in the appendix. If you suspect physical, sexual, mental or emotional abuse or neglect, it is your responsibility to report it. Never assume someone else will or has reported it.

You may not want to make a report for fear that you are mistaken and that no abuse has or is occurring. You may also be afraid the family will know who made the report and will be angry with you. However, the family is not told who made the report at the time of the investigation or at any later date. In fact, the worker who investigates the case seldom knows who made the report. It is also possible to remain anonymous when you make a report. Regardless of your fear, it is still better to make the report so that the abuse can be investigated. Remember, a child's life may be at stake.

> *Regardless of your fear, report all suspected abuse; a child's life may be at stake.*

DFPS only investigates allegations of abuse or neglect on members of the family or those living with the child and for school personnel and volunteers. All other allegations are investigated by law enforcement. When a report is made, an investigator working for the state department is assigned the case. They are responsible for determining if there is cause for concern. DFPS is under strict guidelines about what constitutes abuse or neglect and does not automatically remove all investigated children from their families. The state code concerning these guidelines is quite lengthy. It may be found in its entirety on the Texas state web site. Other states' guidelines will vary and may often be viewed on their respective web sites. A list of each state's human services web address is listed in the appendix.

DFPS may remove a child from his/her home at any time during the investigation if it is determined that the child is in immediate danger or if there is a genuine threat of harm. If the threat or danger can be controlled, the child is left in the home until a relative or absent parent is located with whom the child may be placed. If the threat or danger cannot be controlled, the child is in an emergency situation and is immediately removed and placed in foster care. The search for absent parents or other relatives is made after the child has been removed.

Many foster homes receive children on a temporary basis. They will often only keep the child for a few days until a suitable relative is found. Our first placement was with us only five days before being placed with a relative. In some states, an emergency foster family is on call at all times and even paid to be on call. This is not the case in Texas where any home can be called at any time and no payment is received until the child is in the home. There are also emergency shelters available in some areas where a child can be placed temporarily while awaiting a relative or other placement. These shelters will usually only house a child for up to 30 days. Very young children are only placed in this type of shelter if no other home is available at the time of their removal.

When a child is removed, in Texas and in some other states, the assigned caseworker for the child will contact the Central

Placement Unit (CPU) who will then locate a suitable foster home for the child. In other states, the worker is responsible for finding a suitable home. The foster family is then called and offered the child. If they accept, the child is brought to the home or the family may be asked to collect the child from the state or agency office. If the foster family contacted declines the child, for any reason, the CPU or worker will select another family until one is located, and the child enters that home.

The children who are removed from their homes are not typical healthy children. If they were, they would not have been removed. They have often been abused physically, sexually or emotionally, sometimes the child has suffered a combination of these forms of abuse. They may have also been neglected as well as abused. In some cases, neglect alone caused the removal and no abuse was inflicted on the child. You may believe that a child who has suffered only neglect is not in as bad a condition as one who suffered abuse, but this is not the case. A neglected child has not been cared for as a child should be and can have any number of problems. The problems faced by both abused and neglected children are discussed in Chapter 9: What Are the Greatest Challenges.

All Children are different and cannot be grouped into one common category.

In some cases, an infant may be removed directly from the hospital at the time of its birth. This occurs when the birth mother tests positive for drug use or appears incapable of caring for the infant. If another child has been previously removed from the mother and is still in the foster care system, than an open case file exists and DFPS will be contacted before allowing the infant to leave the hospital. In some cases, the mother will be allowed to take the infant home under close supervision by DFPS, in other cases, the infant will be immediately placed into alternate care, depending on the current situation. We had a placement in our care at the time her sister was born. We were told of her birth, but the infant was allowed to return home with her birth mother. After a few months, she was also removed from her home and placed with us.

Children can come into care at any age from birth through age 17. They can come from a variety of situations and for a variety of reasons. Each child has a unique situation and reason for entering the foster care system. They are also unique in the way in which they have handled their past situation and in the way they will handle the transition to a foster home. Knowing where the child has come from can be of great benefit in caring for the child, but remember that all children are different and unique and cannot be lumped into one common category.

Chapter Four

When the Child Comes

Once you are certified, it is only a matter of time before a child will be placed with you. For some this could be days, for others months. If you carry a cellular phone, you may want to give this as a contact number as well. Our first call was received a couple of weeks after we were certified.

I desperately wanted a placement and jumped every time the phone rang, hoping this would be the call. Surprisingly, when the call finally came, we turned them down. I wasn't sure whether we had made the right decision. I couldn't believe we had turned down our first chance. I wondered if I would ever get another call or had I destroyed my chances by rejecting the first one. I was also upset that I had chosen not to help these children, but my family had discussed the children we would be able to take and one of these children had been older than we had agreed upon. The waiting began again. The next call was only a couple of hours later. This time it was for a child whom we could accept and we did.

When the call finally comes, you may be too excited to think clearly. That is why it is very important to know beforehand the type of child you will accept. Some considerations you may have are age, race, sex, medical conditions, the reason for the removal and how long they will likely be in care. It is handy to keep a note pad by the phone listing these questions and any others you may want to ask before accepting a child. A list of possible questions is provided for you at the end of this book. You can refer to these questions and jot down the answers. Do not rely on your memory for the answers later. You may be excited or anxious when you receive the call and may not remember the answers to your important questions. Writing them down, allows you to refer to them when making your decision. Not all information will be available every time. If you need to discuss the child with your family before you accept, ask for a number so that you may call the worker back. Take as long as you need but remember these children need to be placed quickly. The call will actually come from the Central Placing Unit (CPU). They only have the information they have been given by the worker who picked up the child. They will try to find a placement for the child as quickly as possible. If you tell them you need more time, they will give you that time, but they will continue looking for a placement while you decide. If they find one before you call back you will have to wait for another call. If you miss out on a placement, there will always be others.

Take as long as you need to decide if a child is right for your family, but these children need to be placed quickly.

We received a call from a worker concerning a child while we were out shopping. We were told only the approximate age of the baby, that it was believed to be healthy and the reasons for removal. We were also told that this would probably be a placement lasting only a few days. There was no other information available at this time. At the time we were not even told whether the baby was a boy or a girl. We accepted this baby and he became our first adoption about one year later.

The workers will tell you what they can, but they do not always have the correct information themselves. Placements expected to last a few days could turn into years or even become permanent. Placements expected to be long term, may last only a few days. A healthy child may have serious medical problems and a sick child may become healthy in a short time. If you accept a child and later discover that you cannot continue to care for them, for whatever reason, the child will be moved into another home. However, it is not fair to accept a child hoping their situation will change and thinking that you can always get rid of the child if you decide you do not want them. This is true, but can be very damaging to the child. Try to make the most informed decision possible for your sake as well as that of the child.

Once you have accepted a child, there are more questions you need to ask. You need to know when to expect the child. The worker may be waiting on an available foster home before removing the child, or the child may already be in custody. You may have only a few hours or a couple of days to prepare for the child's arrival. The child may be coming with clothing and other items, or they may be coming with only the clothes they are wearing, which may not be appropriate. The worker will usually tell you what the child has with them if they have this information. They are trying to work quickly and may forget to give you important information. You also need to ask if the child has any allergies, particularly food allergies, and if they are on any medication. Make sure you receive the medication or can easily get it when they arrive.

Hopefully, you have already purchased the necessary items to survive the first few days. If so, you have little to do but wait. If not, you better obtain them quickly. A list, to help you with the preparations, is provided at the end of this book.

As previously mentioned, sometimes the child is brought to your home, other times you may be asked to collect them from CPS or another location. When you receive the child/children make sure you also receive any necessary paperwork from the worker. This includes a "Placement Authorization for Foster Care/Residential Care" and an "Authorization for Medical, Dental, and Psychological Care," at the very least. These forms may have other names in your area, but they serve the same purpose; they show that you are the legal caretaker of the child and that you are authorized to obtain medical and dental care for the child. You will be asked to sign these forms and you will receive a copy for your own records. A third form is the "Discipline Notification." This form explains what kind of discipline is allowed in the home and what kind of discipline you will use. Most importantly, by signing this form, you agree that no form of physical punishment will be used on the child, by you or anyone who is allowed to discipline the child, including school personnel. You may also receive a Medicaid card at this time or it may come later. These forms are very critical. Do not accept a child without them. Remember, you are ultimately responsible for the child and for meeting all necessary requirements. If you do not receive a necessary form, do not give up. Continue to ask for it from whomever you need. If you are unable to obtain a form from the caseworker, try their supervisor or your family caseworker (or case manager).

Now the child is in your home, so what next? The very next thing you should do is take pictures. Do not make this a major ordeal. The child has already had a stressful day just coming to your home. A simple snapshot may be all you need. If you purchased the supplies from the list provided, you should have a camera. A disposable camera will work for this as well. The worker will probably have already taken a picture of the child, but you should take your own anyway. These pictures show the condition of the child when they first come into care. Be sure to photograph any bruises or sores the child has and the clothing and other items they came with. Do not give the child a bath or change the child's clothes until these pictures have been taken! Some bruises may not be noticeable until the child's clothing is removed. These bruises still need to be photographed for the sake of evidence, but you should probably not take these pictures on your own. Taking pictures of a child's private areas is a very sensitive process and should be done by the police in most cases. It must be done quickly so that it can be documented. However, you do not want to traumatize the child so try to make this quick and simple. It may even need to wait until the following

> *You are ultimately responsible for the child and for meeting all necessary requirements.*

day to reduce further trauma to the child. If you notice severe bruising in a private area, consult with the caseworker as to how best to proceed.

It is not uncommon for a child, toddler, or even a baby, to have broken legs, arms or ribs. They may also be severely beaten. Thankfully, none of my children came with these conditions, but many foster children do. I have heard many stories of foster children, even infants that came straight from the hospital in just such condition. Even if they come from a hospital, document all injuries. Pictures are extremely helpful, but you must also write a description of the injury.

Next, you probably want to check the child for lice. The sooner it is caught, the better. If discovered, treat according to the directions that are included with the lice removing medication. Now, you may bathe the child and change his/her clothes if needed. Do not wash or discard these clothes. Place them in a plastic bag and label it with the date and the child's name. If there are allegations of sexual abuse, these clothes may need to be tested. Washing them would destroy the evidence. If clothing is extremely filthy or very ill-fitting, it may also be used as evidence.

Sometimes the child will come with a lot of belongings. Make a list of everything they come with, down to the last pencil or sock. When the child leaves, you will know what to send with them. Do not discard or sell their things. If they are not useable or you do not need or want them, store them until the child's case has completed.

It is a good idea to give the child a tour of your home. Explain your house rules to them as soon as possible. If the child is old enough to read, it may help to have these rules written down for them. Everything is new to them so do not take anything for granted. Many children come with no basic hygiene skills such as bathing and brushing teeth. It will be up to you to teach these over the next few days and weeks. Eating, particularly sitting at a table and using utensils, may also be foreign to some children in care. Try to establish a schedule and stick with it. Structure will ease the transition into your home and can benefit both you and the child.

You will need to enroll the child in school or daycare if appropriate. All foster children of school age must attend school. They may attend either public or private school. If you choose to enroll the child in private school you will be responsible for any costs associated with this choice. Home schooling of foster children is not allowed even if you home school your own children. If you use home schooling with your own children, you will need to contact your local public school to enroll the foster child.

It is also necessary to schedule a doctor appointment as soon as the Medicaid card arrives or as soon as possible if the card was given to you at the time the child was placed. This appointment must be within 30 days of placement. If the child is over 12 months of age, they will also need a dental appointment within 90 days of placement. Do not forget to schedule an evaluation with Early Childhood Intervention (ECI) if the child is under age three. These visits are essential in determining the condition of the child when they first enter care. The child may change dramatically in the first couple of weeks in care so schedule these visits as soon as possible.

Now the real work begins, raising the child. This is the work of teaching the child how to be a part of a family. Each child will have a unique set of challenges. Depending on the child's age and previous circumstances, these challenges can be anything. I am not an expert on the behaviors and challenges you will face, but I will mention a few to give you an idea.

Some children, particularly those with younger siblings, may be used to being the "adult." They will have to be taught that they are the child. They will have responsibilities, but they do not make the decisions any more. They are not responsible for feeding and caring for their younger siblings. Other children will be the exact opposite. They may not know how to do anything for themselves including eating, bathing, and basic hygiene. You will have to teach them how to care for themselves. You may need to demonstrate how to brush their teeth, comb their hair, and eat with utensils.

Children who have been abused may shy away from touch. They may be afraid to open up to you and will have to be taught how to trust and that they are special. Victims of abuse may treat and abuse others the same way they were abused. They will need to be supervised and should not be left alone in a room with other children. Some children may act out violently and must be taught better ways to manage their anger and frustration. Treat them with love and guidance and let them know they are accepted.

Although you are responsible for training the child, there are resources available to help you. These are discussed in Chapter 14: What Resources Are Available. The children in your care, regardless of their challenges, need you to provide for their basic needs. You may assume these needs to be food, clothing and shelter, but they also include structure, guidance and love.

Every month you will have a visit from the child's caseworker. Use these visits to learn more about the child and their case and to inform the worker of any special challenges the child has presented. You should also ask any questions and share any concerns with the worker. They can help you find resources and information. You will probably also need to fill out a report on the child every month. This includes questions concerning illnesses and medication, behavior, educational or treatment progress.

After the first month, you should schedule medical and dental visits at the appropriate times. Each time the child has a physical or dental examination, the doctor or dentist must fill out a form concerning that visit. Your child's caseworker should give you this form before you take them to the doctor, but you may need to remind them. This form is given to the worker as soon as possible to be placed in the child's records.

The child in your care is essentially your child. This means you can take them to church or other activities that your family is involved in. However, there are some rules that must be followed. These rules may vary but every state will have similar rules. You must have permission to take a child out of state. In many areas, this permission must come from a judge, so give plenty of notice to the caseworker for permission to be granted. There are also limits to how long you can be away from home without obtaining permission. You should notify the child's worker any time you are planning to travel.

Respite care may be available for you if you cannot take the child with you when you travel. Respite care is care for the child provided by another foster home for temporary relief. This will depend on the availability of caregivers in your area. Check with your family's caseworker for more information on respite care. Be aware of the child's visits with their families. Try to plan your travel so as not to conflict with these visits. It may be possible to reschedule a particular visit if there is a problem.

You will be in touch with the child's caseworker often and they will discuss what is happening, concerning the case, with you. If you have any questions, ask them. They will supply you with answers if they have them and are able to do so. Sometimes the children will be in your care for only a few short days and you will not have to do all of these things mentioned. However, regardless of what you have been told, proceed as if you will have the child for a long time. It is often easier to cancel appointments than to schedule them. A few days can easily become a few weeks, months, or even longer.

As previously stated, a child may be in your care for a few days up to a few years before their case is settled. Government and bureaucracy can move very slowly. It is often difficult to watch a child be in care for so long not knowing the outcome of their case. If a child is in your care from a very young age, they may not even be aware of their situation. Older children will be more affected by delays in their cases. They may not know how to feel. They do not know where they will be living from one day to the next or who their mom and dad even are. Children will handle these feelings in different ways, be prepared for anything. More is mentioned on these feelings and the challenges they present in Chapter 9: What Are the Greatest Challenges.

When a child enters care, their case is given a dismissal date. In Texas, this date is set for one year from the date the child entered care. This is the date by which the case must be completed. Keep in mind, this date can be changed and extensions can be granted by the judge for an additional six months beyond this date. Further extensions may be granted for extenuating circumstances. Extensions can be granted for any number of reasons. If one or both of the parents are working on their plan, but have not completed it, an extension could be granted to allow them time to complete their plan. In the case of one of our foster children, a conflict of interest developed with one of the attorneys too close to the dismissal date. A new attorney had to be appointed and a six month extension had to be granted.

Even if an extension is not granted, a case may still extend beyond the dismissal date. If the rights of the parents are terminated, they are given a period of time to appeal the termination. The appeal can take another 18 months to be decided. A delay of this sort can leave the child's case open for two to three years, instead of the original one year time frame. A child coming into care as an infant could be three years old; a ten year old could be 13. You can see how this has potential to greatly affect the child. In fact, our delayed case took two and a half years to complete.

In many cases, particularly for older children, the child is placed in permanent managing conservatorship (PMC). This means the child will remain in foster care until they are 18 and graduate from high school. They may remain in the system until they are 22 if they have not graduated high school. At this time, they are considered to have "aged out" of the system. While in PMC, they will never be allowed to return home and they will not be adoptable. If this occurs, you have the choice of having the child live with you or of sending them to another foster home. When the child "ages out" of the system, they may continue to live in your home if you agree, but they will be considered to be an adult in your home. You will no longer receive a reimbursement for them and you may need to move them out of your other children's room which is decided on an individual basis.

There is no sure way to know when a case will end or how long the child will remain in your care. Be prepared to care for the child for the duration of their case whether that is one day or 18 years. In the next chapter, I will discuss what is involved with providing that care.

Chapter Five

How Busy Will You Be

One of the most important things you will need is a calendar. If you do not have one, get one now! I suggest you obtain one with a lot of room to write. You will need to keep track of all meetings, visits, court hearings, doctor appointments, etcetera, for each child in your care. The calendars with separate lines for each member of your family can be especially helpful. You may also need a travel-sized calendar to keep with you when you are away from the house. Handheld devices such as Personal Digital Assistant's (PDA's), work well for this purpose.

One of the events to list on your calendar is the Permanency Planning Team meeting, otherwise known as PPT meetings. These meetings are conducted at regular intervals beginning shortly after a child is placed in your care. Everyone involved with the child's case is invited to attend the PPT meeting. This can include the child's caseworker, supervisors, biological parents, foster parents, the Court Appointed Special Advocate (CASA) worker for the child, and any other involved parties. CASA will be explained in Chapter 13: Who Else Will Be Involved.

The PPT meeting is a very important meeting. Just as the name suggests, this meeting is used to discuss the child's permanency plan. This permanency plan can and usually does begin as a plan for reunification with the biological parents. If this fails, the plan can be changed to adoption by a relative, adoption by a non-relative, or permanent managing conservatorship. Any and all progress made by the biological parents is discussed at this meet-

How Busy Will You Be

ing, along with further actions that are necessary for reunification. It is a chance for all involved parties to meet and share information to make sure no one is left uninformed.

These meetings are a foster parent's best chance, and in some cases, only chance to provide input concerning the child and their case. It is also one of the best ways to stay informed about the cases of the children in your care. In many areas it may be possible to be connected through a conference call if you are unable to attend. The children are generally not allowed in this meeting. Exceptions can be made for children too young to understand the conversation. Some of the information discussed could hurt the children involved, if they were to hear it.

The same can be said about the court hearings. The children, even the young ones, can not attend unless they have something to add. If you attend the court hearings, you will likely not be invited to speak. You are there as an observer only. There is often information revealed at court hearings you may not have heard before. If you have something you feel needs to be said in court, talk to the child's caseworker or CASA worker before court. Do this as early as you can, to avoid problems. They will advise you on how to proceed.

The children may or may not have visitation with one or both of their biological parents. They may also have visits with their biological siblings. These visits may be regular or occasional; they may be biweekly, weekly, monthly or otherwise. Depending on the current location of the biological parents, the Child Protective Services office, and your location, the children may have to be taken to another city for their visits. You, the foster parent, are responsible for transporting the children to these visits. It may be possible to have transport assistance if you are not able to do it yourself.

Some children who come into care have severe medical conditions and may require frequent doctor visits. Even those who do not have severe medical conditions will need to visit the doctor and dentist regularly. As soon as the Medicaid card is issued, the child must be taken to a physician for a check-up. Regular check-ups are required of all children after the initial check-up. All children older than 12 months must have biannual dental check-ups as well. It is a good idea to know which doctors you will be using before you receive your first placement. Verify that the doctor and dentist you choose will accept Medicaid. If they do not, you will need to find another doctor or expect to pay the fees on your own.

If you will be caring for children under the age of three, you will need to be familiar with Early Childhood Intervention (ECI). This is a service provided for children who need special services for delays or disabilities. They provide services such as speech therapy, physical therapy, occupational therapy, nutrition guidelines, and many others. The local public school system takes over at age three. The public school provides services for older children as well. If you suspect any developmental problems in children under age three, contact ECI for an evaluation as soon as possible. ECI will come to your home for evaluations and therapy sessions. For older children, contact the school for assistance. The school programs will likely take place in a school environment.

If you will have school age children in your care, consider the activities they will be involved in. All extracurricular activities take up time with practice and events. If you plan to let the children in your care participate in them, plan to spend a lot of time transporting children to and from these activities and supporting the child in them.

You will also be spending a lot of time with visits to your home. Each child has a caseworker who is required to visit the child, in your home, every month. These visits usually do not take up much time but plan for at least an hour for each caseworker. If you have several children in your care with different caseworkers, one caseworker may occassionally visit on behalf of the others. These visits give you an opportunity to discuss any concerns or questions you have concerning the child. This is also a chance for the caseworker to observe your interaction with the child.

Each foster family is assigned a foster home developer. This is a caseworker for your family. Private agencies may call this

How Busy Will You Be

person a case manager. They are responsible for keeping track of your training hours and insuring that you are meeting all requirements as a foster parent according to the Minimum Standards guidelines. If you have a problem with a caseworker, this is the person to whom you should report your problems to. State workers are required to visit in your home every quarter, or every three months.

If you plan to care for several children, your schedule will be even more crowded.

Private agencies visit more frequently and may visit in your home twice monthly and by phone or other communications twice monthly. This frequency means they will consume more of your time, but will also be more available and develop a closer relationship with you.

As an example, assume you have two foster children in your home and for our purposes, they have separate caseworkers. Every month you will have two separate visits from caseworkers. If you are with a private agency, you will also have two visits from your worker. This is a total of four visits, in your home, each month. Add to this any doctor appointments, therapy sessions and parent visits for each child. Also, add an extra-curricular activity for each child. Each activity adds its own schedule of practices. It is easy to see how quickly your calendar will fill up each month. If you plan to care for more children than this, remember your schedule will be even more crowded.

Training is another time consuming matter. If you are certified for basic care, you currently need 20 hours of training annually. For therapeutic homes, the requirement is 50 hours annually. These hours must include four hours of discipline training per adult, HIV training, and training on psychotropic drugs. These training requirements are for Texas at the time of this writing, other states may vary in their requirements.

The following is an accurate example, of the time involved, taken from my own calendar. July 1: Rehabilitation therapy for a foster child in a nearby city involving two hours of travel plus one hour for the appointment. July 13th: Speech therapy for another child in care, one hour. July 14: ECI (early childhood intervention) visit to discuss speech therapy for the child, one hour. July 15: CPR renewal training, all morning. July 21: Foster home caseworker visit, one hour. July 26: Doctor Appointment with a specialist in another city, one hour appointment, three and a half hours travel. July 27: Well child visit for one child, one hour. July 28: ECI visit again, one hour. July 29: Caseworker visit, one hour. Not all months are as busy as this one was, but depending on the needs of the individual children in your care, they can be much busier.

Another time consuming, yet well worth it activity, is Preparation-for-Adult-Living Services (PALS). This is a service provided for teenagers at least 16 years of age who will likely remain in foster care until they are 18. It is designed to prepare them for adult living. Those under the age of 21 who were in foster care until they turned 18 are also accepted. They are taught how to balance a checkbook, fill out an application, basic job skills, personal health and many other necessary skills. This is a program that takes place on weekends and evenings. You will be responsible for ensuring the child attends these training classes.

Chapter Six

What You Need to Know About Court

Court is one of the most crucial aspects of foster parenting. This is where every major decision concerning the child is made. The judge alone determines what happens to the child. His or her decision is made based on information presented in court and in the child's file. The judge's own experiences, opinions, and beliefs will also play a role. Because of the importance of court, there is a need for foster parents to understand the court system as it relates to a child.

The decision to remove a child from their home must be confirmed by the court. If possible, DFPS will go before the judge to seek permission to remove a child. If this is not possible, the case is heard immediately (on the first business day) following the removal. At this time, the judge determines whether grounds do indeed exist to warrant the removal of the child or if they should be returned home. If grounds exist, the child remains in care. The next hearing is the 14-day hearing. This hearing takes place within 14 days of the removal. This hearing is to determine whether the child should remain in care or if the immediate concern is no longer present. The biological parents of the child may attend this hearing to defend themselves.

The next hearing is the 60-day status hearing. A status hearing updates the judge on the status of the child in care and all other involved parties. The judge approves the service plan at this hearing. The judge will ensure that services have been set up. An initial permanency hearing is scheduled at five months. This hearing begins the process of determining the child's permanent placement. Status of the case and all involved parties is reviewed. A second permanency hearing is scheduled at nine months, and every 4 months thereafter until permanency is achieved. After permanency has been achieved, placement reviews are held every 6 months until the child is no longer under DFPS care.

You should be notified of all cases concerning the child in your care by the caseworker. When you are notified of a court date, you will also be given the time to appear. You may need to ask the caseworker for this information. This time is the time court is scheduled to begin for all cases, not just the child in your care. If there are several cases being heard that day, you may not know exactly when yours will be called. The order is determined by many factors. There may be conflicts causing a need for one case to take precedence over another, or they may just be called in a scheduled order. You should be there at the time you have been given, but be prepared to wait if your case is not first in line to be heard. You will need to bring something to occupy you during this time such as a book or magazine. If the child is old enough, they will be required to attend court as well.

A trial is held at the conclusion of the case and must be held on or before the date set for dismissal of the case. This date is one year from the time the child came into CPS custody. In some cases, an extension may be granted allowing another six months before dismissal of the case. An extension will be asked for if the department feels it is necessary. The decision to grant the extension will be made by the judge if there is an acceptable reason for the extension. If this occurs, the trial will be held prior to the new dismissal date set by the court.

If either or both of the parents have signed a relinquishment of rights, the judge will rule on that relinquishment at the time of the trial. He must accept the relinquishment for it to be legal. The mother of the child may not know who the child's father is. If no known father exists, the judge may terminate the rights of an "unknown father" at this time. Their must be a legal termination of rights for the father of the child to avoid any possible future claims to the child. Evidence must be presented to show that every effort was made to locate the father, by the department. If the parents of the child are known and do not relinquish their rights, the trial proceeds. When all parties are in agreement, the trial is relatively short. This usually occurs when DFPS desires to return the child to their biological home.

When DFPS wishes to terminate the rights of one or both parents, the trial may be lengthy because they must prove that the parent is not suitable, according to the family code. The department may use any of the points, listed in the state code, to attempt to prove their case. In order for parental rights to be terminated, the judge must agree with at least two of these points. Both sides may have as many witnesses as they choose. You, as the foster parent, may be asked to testify at this trial as well. All witnesses are named at the beginning of the trial. All witnesses, other than those who are parties to the suit, are asked to leave the court room. If you are among these witnesses, you will also have to leave the court room. You must remain at the courthouse in the designated area so that you will be ready whenever called. You will not be allowed to discuss the case with anyone during this time. You will take your breaks when the court does because you will not likely know when you will be called in. There should be breaks for bathroom and lunch given at reasonable times.

When attending court, bring something along to read or do while you wait.

Contested cases may take a long time. I was a witness at a termination trial for the parents of one of the children in my care that took an entire day. We began at 9:00 a.m. and I was not called until nearly 4:00 p.m. It is possible for a trial of this nature to be even longer. Remember to bring something along to read or do while you wait so that the time will pass more quickly.

When you are called you will take the stand to answer questions. There are several people who will be asking questions at this time, the DFPS attorney, the parent's individual attorneys, the child's appointed attorney, and CASA. You may be asked questions by any or all of these parties.

It is important to dress and act appropriately when appearing in court. Always look professional. This means you should dress in nice clothes such as dress pants, ties or dresses. I was once given the advice of: "Look better than the other side." You want to be taken seriously if you take the stand and you want the judge to see you as a responsible and professional witness or guardian of the child. If you are in the courtroom, the judge will see you. It is generally noted that you are in attendance at court.

If you are a witness, it is crucial that you dress and act professionally. Do not get angry or out of control in the court room. Emotional outbreaks do not help you. It is best to speak clearly and answer all questions truthfully.

At the conclusion of the trial, the judge will rule. They may rule that termination of parental rights is in the best interest of the child. They may also rule that there are insufficient grounds to terminate the rights. If this ruling is made, the judge has two options. He may rule that the child be returned to either or both of the parents, or he may rule that the state be given permanent custody of the child. In this case, the child does not return home, but they are not freed for adoption.

If the parental rights are terminated, the parents then have the right to request an appeal. They have 30 days from the date DFPS files the termination to appeal. A date for the appeal hearing should be set at the trial. The appeal hearing provides an opportunity for the judge to change his mind. If the judge determines that he/she was wrong to terminate the rights, they can reverse their decision at this time. If the parents have decided to appeal, the judge is given the opportunity to hear their reasons for appeal and then either grant or deny the appeal. The judge will decide whether the appeal is frivolous or non-frivolous. If the judge rules that the appeal is non-frivolous, it will proceed. The parents will be assigned new attorneys.

What You Need to Know About Court

The appeal can then take place in one of two ways. A review of the trial may be requested in which the record of the trial is reviewed by a review board that may uphold or overturn the judge's decision. Another method for the appeal is to have a new trial. If this method is selected, a new trial will be held in front of a different judge. This trial will not be held immediately. It will be scheduled and you will be informed of the new date and time.

If the judge rules that the appeal is frivolous, the case is not over. Because an appeal was filed with the court, the Court of Appeals must rule on it as well; however, this does not automatically happen. The legal department of CPS is required to file a notice of appeal with the Court of Appeals. The parent or parents whose rights were terminated are given a chance to continue their appeal. The court does not assign a new attorney in this situation because the appeal was ruled as frivolous, but the appealing parent may furnish their own attorney and pay for the review of the trial. The parents have a limited set time period to decide to continue the appeal after the notice has been filed with the court. At this time, the Court of Appeals will rule on this case. It can take several months for the case to be heard by the court. Once this ruling has been made, there is a further waiting period to allow the decision to be contested before a mandate can be issued by the court. After all of this has occurred, the child is finally free for adoption. Adoption is discussed thoroughly in Chapter 12: How Do You Adopt from the System.

It is important to be patient during the appeal time, but make sure the process is continuing. Often times caseworkers are overloaded and important processes are sometimes overlooked. As an example, we had a case go to termination for one of our children. The court appointed attorney was released when the appeal, filed by one of the parents, was ruled to be frivolous. The CPS legal team neglected to file the notice of appeal with the Court of Appeals and the process was stalled. We had our attorney look into the delay. He discovered this oversight and informed CPS, who began working on this problem at this time. This situation was resolved, but had we not gotten our attorney involved, it could have been a much greater delay than it actually was. In this particular case, the caseworker herself was not aware of the reason for the delay until after we became involved. Do not assume that they always know what is happening. If your questions are not being answered to your satisfaction, it is your duty to find the answers.

Chapter Seven

Who is the Child's Best Advocate

In your initial training, you will most likely be taught that you are the child's advocate. Not only are you the child's advocate, but you must also be the child's best advocate because you have direct contact with the child and know them best. You know what works and does not work with them. You know their likes and dislikes. Because of this, it is crucial that you stay informed about the child's case. You need to know everything you can so that you can better help the child. If you feel something is not being handled properly with regards to the child's case, with their school education or any other aspect of their care, it is your responsibility to do something about it.

The caseworkers and all others working within the system are quite often overloaded. This can lead to mistakes being made that will affect the child in your care. Sometimes paperwork is not properly filed or other issues are not conducted in a timely manner. If something seems to be taking longer than it should there may be a mistake involved. If you are unsure, ask the caseworker. If the answer you are given is unclear or if the question is not answered to your satisfaction, ask again. Ask the caseworker for clarification. If you do not get the answer you need, try asking someone else. The caseworker's supervisor may be able to better answer the question. Often, the question must be asked of another department or government office.

We had a child in our care in need of a paternity test. After a couple of months, the child had still not been tested. We asked the caseworker about the test and were told it was out of her hands. She had turned in the paperwork and it was now up to the Attorney General's office to test the child. I contacted the Attorney General's office and was informed that no request had been made. Apparently there was a glitch in the system and the request had never been processed. I informed the caseworker who was then able to remedy the problem and the child was tested. This is not an isolated event. We have had to involve our attorney in various cases as well. In each of these situations a mistake had been made. No one knew it existed until we pursued it. If we had sat back and waited as we were told to do by the caseworkers, these problems could have delayed the children's cases even further.

Being a foster parent is not about making friends. I'm not suggesting you should try to make enemies of all parties involved in the child's case, but you must advocate for the child. Sometimes a worker's feelings may be hurt or you may inconvenience someone, but the child must come first. Sometimes, the best thing to do is to be patient, but don't wait unnecessarily. First be sure you know why you are waiting and that all things have been properly handled.

Court and PPT meetings provide excellent opportunities to advocate for the children in our care. At PPT meetings, the foster parents are given an opportunity to voice any concerns they have. Be prepared for this time and bring along a list of questions or concerns to be addressed. The list is recommended so that nothing is forgotten during this meeting. Foster parents are not usually allowed to speak in court; however exceptions may be made if the attorney for the department is notified of any concerns in advance. Another way to advocate for the child in court is by notifying the Court Appointed Special Advocate (CASA) about any concerns you have. CASA workers are discussed in detail in Chapter 13: Who Else Will Be Involved. Just attending the Court hearings and PPT meetings shows your support for the child. Remember the words of

> *" I would go to any of these things for my own child, wouldn't I?"*

one foster parent who stated, "I'd go to any of these things for my own child, wouldn't I?"

Another place you should be an advocate for your foster child is with their education. If your foster child has special education needs, you need to make sure they receive the necessary assistance. When a child is in need of special education services, the school must provide these services if the child is over age three. The planning meetings, to determine their needs, are called Admission, Review, and Dismissal (ARD) meetings. The parents of special needs children are members of the ARD team. Since a foster child is a ward of the state, or under the state's control, he or she is provided with a surrogate parent. This surrogate parent can be anyone who will take on the role of the parent in the ARD planning meetings. The foster parent is not automatically assigned this role. If you want to be the designated surrogate parent, you must let the school know at the time the ARD is scheduled. The school can designate you as the surrogate parent, and is required to unless they have a good reason not to designate you. You will then have to complete a surrogate parent training within 90 days of obtaining this designation. As the child's foster parent, you are most suited for this role, but again don't assume it will be automatically assigned to you. In some school districts, it is not necessary to take these steps to become the surrogate parent.

Be aware of your foster child's progress in school and other activities. You cannot know when to step in and advocate for the child if you are not aware of their activities and involvement. Just as with parenting your own children, you must be involved in the child's life. It is unfair to expect the child in your care to tell you when you need to step in. Many children in foster care have spent much of their lives taking care of themselves. They do not know that it is okay to ask for help. Many do not know or believe that someone would actually care enough about them to help.

Be sure the foster child is given the proper medical care and therapy he or she needs. This can sometimes require a great amount of effort on your part. When a child initially enters your care, you must have them evaluated by ECI if under age three or by the school if you feel there is a need for special services. Sometimes a child who clearly has a problem or disability does not qualify for services. If this happens, you must advocate for the child once again by finding them the services they need. Many areas, or nearby cities, have private rehabilitation centers that can evaluate the child in specialized areas such as speech, audiology and physical therapy. Medicaid will cover these services and a child may be accepted for therapy there that is not accepted anywhere else. If all else fails, you need to become an expert in whatever area the problem lies. There are books and other resources available for most problems children face, you just need to find them.

> *"Always stand up for what you think is right"*

One of the best ways to advocate for your foster child is by showing them that you care about them and what is going on in their lives. They need to know that you are willing to help them and that you will gladly help when needed. But they must also learn that you will advocate for them even if they do not ask for help. The only way to show this is to know what is going on in their lives and where they might need help. Remember what a surveyed foster parent said, "Always stand up for what you think is right" because if you don't, who will? And from another foster parent, "If helping these kids is truly in your heart, you'll seek the training, get support, ask all the questions you need answers to and won't give up. You'll be a strong advocate for your children."

Chapter Eight

When a Child Goes Home

Happiness, sadness, joy, fear and anger are just some of the emotions that may be experienced by the child or the foster parent when a child goes home. When a child leaves your care, they may be going back to live in the home from which they were removed from or to live with another relative such as an aunt or uncle, grandparents, a sister or a brother. The child may be leaving to go into a non-relative adoptive home, or even into another foster home or they may have simply "aged out" of the system. Regardless of where they are going, this will be an emotional time.

When people learn I am a foster parent, the statement I hear most often is, "I could never give the child back. How do you do it?" My response to this question has always been "I don't know. I haven't done it yet." That is not entirely true, but it is pretty close. To date, we have only had one child leave us. It was our first placement, and the child was only with us for five days. The child had been a very sweet child and I still think about him sometimes. That child impacted me tremendously in only five days. I consider any child in my care to be one of my kids. I know the reality is that they may leave at any time, but when a child lives in your home as one of your children, it is sometimes difficult to remember they are someone else's child.

I have often said the hardest part of foster parenting is having a child leave. Because I have not personally experienced this yet, and will not likely ever experience this, I will rely on the experiences of other foster parents for the purposes of this chapter.

Our experience is not typical of foster parenting, most experience a much higher rate of children leaving their homes so be prepared to have many of the children you care for leave at some time. If adoption is your primary goal, having a child leave can be especially difficult. Take the wise advice of one foster/adoptive mother, "Go in planning to help children, not looking to build a family; that comes in time. Helping the family reunite can be very rewarding."

When a child does leave they will experience many strong emotions. The child may be excited to be leaving or they may be angry. Even if the child wants to go to this particular home, they may have mixed emotions about leaving you, the foster parent. You have had the role of parenting them throughout their case. You may even be the only parent they have ever known. When you first find out the child is going to a new home, you need to start preparing them. Make this a positive transition for the child. Tell them the positive features of their new home. Do not let any negative emotions and feelings you have affect the child's perception of the change. Even if you think this change is not in the child's best interest, find something positive to discuss with the child. They may be getting a permanent home or reuniting with family members. They may be going to see old friends or they may be meeting a new family that they can get to know.

Sometimes these transitions occur very quickly, other times you may have several weeks or even months to prepare. There may be visits to the new home before the actual transition is made. These can help the child adjust to their future home, but they may also make some situations worse. The foster child may start to revert to past behaviors such as bed wetting and acting out. If this happens, try to help them past their fear, anger, or whatever emotion they are struggling with. Be sure to notify the caseworker of any behavioral changes during this time, it could be a sign of a real problem with the new environment. At the same time you are trying to help them accept their new home, don't forget that they still live with you. Do not get overly positive about the change or the child may start to feel that you never wanted them to live with you and that you are happy to see them go. It can be difficult to find the right balance, but for your sake and that of the child, you must try.

During all this time, you and the rest of your family are going to be experiencing strong emotions of your own. Having a child, that you have loved and cared for, leave is one of the hardest aspects of foster parenting. These emotions can be so strong that one foster mother compared it to death saying, "Prepare for the separation when the kids leave…it's unreal pain. I feel as if two of my own children died." Your own emotions may not be this strong, but you will feel a sense of loss. There are ways to prepare for this loss.

Even though we have not had this experience, while foster parents, we reminded ourselves often that the children we cared for could go home at any time. We also reminded our oldest child that the foster children could leave at any time. We didn't want him to be caught by surprise if one of them were to leave. If you have other children in your home, it is important that they are aware of the temporary nature of foster care. An older child will remember this better, but may still develop deep relationships with the new children. Don't let them be caught by surprise when a child leaves, but don't make your foster child feel as if they don't belong because they are only temporary. Like the foster child, your own children may experience behavior changes. Try not to overreact to these changes, but handle them as you would any other challenges. It may even be necessary to see a counselor for help during this time.

A friend of mine, who is also a foster parent, has experienced this loss. She had a baby in her care for a couple of months who was then returned to its mother. This was not a good environment for the child, but there was nothing that could be done on her part. This was very difficult for her. She struggled with whether she could handle having this happen again. She debated quitting foster parenting at the time. She asked me a very important question that I feel needs answering at this time. She asked, "How do you not attach to the child? How can you keep from getting your heart broken?" My answer was simply "You can't". For the sake of the child and your family, you have to attach to the child. You have to love the child and with this love, comes the risk that yes, you will get your heart broken. The good news is that hearts can heal and there will be another child to love.

Unfortunately, there will always be another child. There are so many children needing loving homes right now and there are not enough homes for them to go to. Because of this, many of these children continue to suffer. Don't give up and quit just because a child leaves your home. There are too many children in desperate need of good loving foster homes to lose a foster home every time a heart gets broken. Continue to love the children and continue to give them a place to come to where they can be loved and touch someone's heart.

> *A case may suddenly change, and what you once knew to be true may no longer be true.*

Yes, foster parenting is emotional, but it is important to remember why we do what we do. The primary and initial permanency plan for all foster children is reunification. The state would like to eventually return all children that are removed from their homes back to those homes. Because of this, most foster parents experience a higher turnover rate than we did.

I know other foster parents who have had approximately half of their placements leave. Others seldom have one stay for very long. Some foster parents only take in children on a short term basis. Others may keep them permanently. Regardless of the amount of time you intend a child to stay in your care, you must prepare yourself for their departure. If you want to adopt children, this can be especially hard as was the case with my friend. Even if you don't intend to keep the children permanently, you will still experience feelings of loss when a child you have learned to love and have cared for, for a time, leaves.

Because we, as foster parents, don't know how long a child will stay with us, there are several things we must do. I have already mentioned the need to remind yourself and your children that the child could leave at any time. This is very crucial to your state of mind. I want to stress again to be careful not to harm the foster child. They need to know they are loved and not be made to think that you can't wait until they leave. Remember, a case may suddenly change, and what you once knew to be true, may no longer be true. We had a child come to us whose mother willingly gave her to the state, not intending to take her back. We thought there was a good chance we would be keeping this child. Later, the parents began to work the permanency plan and do what they had been told was required to get their child back. At this point, we felt we would lose this child. Later, the mother willingly gave up her rights and the father's rights were terminated. By this time, we had given up trying to figure out whether or not the child would stay with us. This is very confusing to us as adults so imagine how confusing it is to your children.

Another step we can take to prepare for a child leaving is to make a scrapbook for that child. The state of Texas actually requires you to create a life book, but many foster parents never get around to it. This scrapbook, or life book, is very important for both your family and the foster child. It provides a record of the time the child was with you. When the child is older, they need to be able to look back and remember their time with you and not be left with huge gaps in their childhood. A child, who is passed around between several foster homes, may not remember many of their placements. A young child may have the same problem so at the very least you should send pictures with the child of their time with you. If this is all you send, be sure to write a description on the back of each picture. A better idea is to make a scrapbook or memory book. Scrapbooking is a very popular hobby today and it is easy to learn. If you are a scrapbooker, this should be easy for you. If not, there are many places to learn about scrapbooking. The scrapbook can be as simple or as elaborate as you choose. You can stick a picture in it with a short description or you can group and decorate your pictures. I recommend that you make two memory books or make copies of each page so that you may retain a copy as well.

In some cases, you may need to send the copy and not the original if it is likely to be destroyed in the home they will be returning to. Having two copies of the memory book will provide that the child will always have a record of their stay with you and you will always have a record of them.

Long before the child goes home, you can develop a relationship with the biological parents. This is not always possible, but when allowed it can prove very useful when the child goes home. Begin this step by not judging the biological parents too harshly. This is often hard because of the terrible things they have done to the child, but it is often helpful to remember that the parents are often only continuing the cycle of abuse and neglect. They were often victims of abuse and neglect themselves and may in fact be products of the system. At least two of the biological mothers of my children fell into this category. They were abused themselves and had in one case been placed in the care of a relative for a time.

> *The parents of foster children are often only continuing the cycle of abuse*

This doesn't excuse their behavior, but it can help you to understand why they did what they did to their own children. You may have the opportunity to meet the parents at PPT meetings, at court hearings and at visitations. Try to develop a friendship with the parents, even if only a casual friendship. A surveyed foster parent said, "Be kind to families – you want to be there, if allowed, later."

It is possible to remain a part of the child's life after they go home. If you have formed a relationship with the biological parents, you may be allowed to see the children on occasion. Some foster parents have become mentors to the parents and are able to provide a valuable resource to them after the child returns home. This enabled them to remain a part of the child's life. Regardless of future involvement with the child, you must try your best to make the transition back home as easy as possible for yourself and for the child.

Chapter Nine

What are the Greatest Challenges

The foster parents I surveyed were asked what challenges they faced as foster parents. Many answered "dealing with CPS" and "challenges with CPS." Several others mentioned problems with workers. From paperwork to personalities, there are plenty of opportunities for challenges created by the state system.

One of the most common challenges for foster parents is working with caseworkers. Caseworkers are just like everyone else in the world which means that there are good workers and bad workers. There are those who want to help you and the children and those who consider casework just another job. Even good caseworkers can have bad days. If you have a problem with a caseworker, talk to them about it. This is the best method to avoid misunderstandings. If you cannot work out your problems, speak to the caseworker's supervisor. The caseworker does not live in your home so they do not witness all of the behaviors you see in the children. They may feel that any problems you are having are your fault and not the child's. If this is the case, the burden of proof will lie with you.

Caseworkers can be difficult to contact. Many are overloaded with cases and are seldom in their offices. Because they work for a state agency, they are often overloaded with duties and paperwork. Some workers handle thirty, forty, fifty and even more cases depending on their position within the agency. Getting answers to your questions and voicing your concerns may take time. One solution is to be aware of the many methods of possible communication with the caseworker. If you have difficulty contacting the worker by telephone, leave a message for them. You can also email your questions or concerns. This method allows the worker to reply when they get a chance. You may get a quicker response because you do not have to locate them at a specific time. I have found that email is much more effective than phone communication. Email also provides you with a record of the question or concern in writing. Save any email that you write or receive concerning foster care. They may prove useful later. If time is not an issue, send the worker a note in the mail, but as with email, save a copy of any correspondence. Any or all of these methods of communication may work for you. Determine what works best for your situation, but remember to be flexible.

Determine what works best for your situation, but be flexible.

Another concern, when working with the state, is the availability of information. As a foster parent, you will probably want to know as much as possible about the child's case. This knowledge can help you better understand what the child needs and how to prepare yourself and the child for what might happen concerning their case. This information is often difficult to obtain. Some caseworkers will help you fill in the blanks with this knowledge. Others will tell you little or nothing concerning the child's case. Asking questions is the best way to obtain information. Keep in mind that the worker may not be legally able to answer some of your questions. If you are not able to obtain the information you need from the caseworker, there are other methods you can use. One of these methods is to attend all PPT meetings and court hearings you are able to attend. Much of the information about the case you need to know is discussed at these meetings and hearings. You can ask questions at PPT meetings, but not at court hearings. Sometimes caseworkers will give you incorrect information. They will tell you what they know or think at the time, but they may not have all the facts themselves. If you appear to have been given incorrect information, ask them again at a later date.

In an ideal world, a child would have one caseworker for the duration of their case, but this is often not the case. The turnover rate among workers is very high. Many workers burn out and leave casework completely. Some transfer to other departments or other offices. A worker may retire or be let go or even be fired. Strong differences of opinion between a worker and the foster family may cause a new worker to be assigned. Any number of reasons can cause the child to be assigned a new caseworker. I have personally experienced three of these reasons. In just slightly over a year, one of the children in my care had four different workers. This change creates many challenges. One of the biggest challenges is that the new worker is not as familiar with the child's case. To make this transition to a new worker as smooth as possible, you should be as informed as you can be concerning the child's case. You will then be able to assist the new worker with any gaps in their knowledge concerning the case.

Each child's caseworker must visit with you and the child in your home every month. You may glance at your calendar one day and realize that the month is already half over and none of the caseworkers have scheduled their monthly visits yet. This happens more often than it should. I try to contact each of my workers at this time, to schedule their visits. I often receive responses including statements such as: "I can't believe it's that time already." And "I'm glad you reminded me." I typically use email for these reminders as that allows us to quickly communicate back and forth to select a date. You may even want to make a note on your calendar reminding you to call the workers.

Challenges faced when working with the state are not limited to caseworkers. There is a lot of paperwork that has to be completed. When the child visits the doctor or dentist, the medical provider must complete a form that you then return to the caseworker. Every month, a synopsis of the child's good and bad behavior, education, and medical problems, must be filled out. Usually the caseworker will give you a form for this purpose. Some regions will reimburse you for travel to parent visits, medical visits and meetings. If you are lucky to be offered this reimbursement and wish to receive it, you must fill out a form for it as well. In our case, we fill out the form and mail it to our worker. She writes up a new form and sends it back to us to sign and then we mail it on to another office. A few weeks later we receive the reimbursement.

If you wish to travel out of state, country, or in some areas even out of the county you reside in, you will need permission. We request permission from the caseworker, who fills out the necessary paperwork, to be signed by the judge who controls the child's case. Individual states and counties vary on these rules. It is also necessary to ask permission if you will be traveling away from home for more than 72 hours in Texas. It is customary, and in some places required, to tell the caseworker any time you will be traveling so they can be aware of the child's location.

Another challenge is that you are often not allowed to raise the child how you feel they should be raised. The state and birth parents have some control in these matters. In many states, physical discipline of any kind is not allowed. If you are in the habit of using physical discipline with your own children, you must remember that the foster children have a different set of rules. Because they are not your children, you are under strict guidelines as to their care and discipline. It is often necessary to receive permission from the birth parents for things that you may feel should be your right as the caregiver to decide. One of these issues is cutting or altering the child's hair. Even a simple trim may not be allowed. Many cultures do not believe in cutting the child's hair, or a parent may not want their child's hair to be cut or trimmed for any number of reasons. Always be sure to ask before you cut the child's hair. It is often only necessary for you to ask the caseworker, who will check with the parents, once and be given permission at that time for any future haircuts as well. Similar problems occur when a child's ears are pierced without parental permission. Do not make any physical changes to the child without obtaining permission.

> *Foster children have a different set of rules.*

This different set of rules can create many problems for you and your family. It is difficult to tell the foster child that they cannot do something that your own child is doing. How do you explain to a foster child that they have to stay with someone else while the rest of your family takes a vacation simply because you were not able to obtain permission for them to travel? The child cannot be given as much freedom as your own child because nearly everything they do must be approved by their caseworker.

Medicaid provides its own unique challenge. Medicaid is a valuable resource that is further described in Chapter 14: What Resources Are Available, but it can be a hassle to work with. The Medicaid card must state a medical or dental visit is needed in order for you to take the child in for a regular exam. Occasionally the card does not list this information. We encountered this problem with one of our children. She turned two and needed her check-up, but her card did not state that the medical visit was needed, so the doctor could not see her. I could not take her for the visit and pay for it myself because that would be considered fraudulent. If you can afford to take the child to the doctor, the child shouldn't be on Medicaid. Since the foster child qualifies automatically that is not necessarily the case, but it was still not a legal option. I contacted the Medicaid number listed on the back of the card and was told it would appear on the next card, but because the system was run by a computer no one could alter what the card said. The next month's card came, but the statement was still not on it. After repeated calls to Medicaid, I gave up and took her for a different type of visit that the doctor could bill to Medicaid. Seven months later, the card finally said she was due for an appointment. Had I waited until the card said that, I would have been in violation, as a foster parent, because the child had not had a regular physical examination. If you encounter this situation, there is little you can do. Make the caseworker aware of the situation and contact Medicaid so you are on record as attempting to fulfill this obligation. Make the contact with the caseworker in writing such as with email so that you have proof of it if necessary. After that, your only course of action is to wait and hope the next card is correct.

Another challenge all foster parents encounter is the physical, emotional and medical condition of the children. Many foster parents mentioned children were not leveled properly and had severe discipline and medical problems. The children in care do not come from good healthy homes. Many of them have serious medical conditions and if you become certified for therapeutic care, you may have some of these children in your care. These are the children who have known medical, psychological, and physical disabilities. The extra required training for therapeutic care will help you cope with these problems. There are also many resources available to you, which are discussed in detail in Chapter 14: What Resources Are Available.

The challenge with many of these conditions is that they are not always easily recognizable. Quite often, the children who are placed as basic care children also have these problems. They may be milder and therefore more difficult to detect. It is possible for a child to be diagnosed after they are in your care. We had a child come into our home as a basic care child. She had some emotional problems that concerned us. We later discovered she had Fetal Alcohol Syndrome (FAS). This is a condition that can have serious medical, physical, and emotional repercussions. No one knew she had anything to be concerned with, at the time of placement.

You need to be aware that any child can have almost any problem and it may not be known until after they are placed with you. The problems they have may not even surface for several years. There are several common problems that occur more frequently with the children in foster care. These will be briefly described, but remember these are only a few of the possible problems the children may have.

Hoarding food is a problem faced by many foster parents. Many of the children in care have been severely neglected and starved. As a result, they may have difficulty adjusting to having food regularly available. Some may be constantly hungry for a few days or even weeks. Others may fear the food will be taken away. These children resort to hoarding. They may sneak food into their rooms and hide it. They want to ensure that they will not starve again. To counter this problem, you should talk to the child. Let them know that they will always be fed. Don't withhold food from them as punishment (this form of punishment should not be used on any child and its use is forbidden by CPS). Even after talking with the child, they may still hoard food. You may want to allow them to keep some foods in their room for security. Be sure to explain which foods are acceptable and which are not. It may also be necessary for you to check their room periodically for hidden food. Counseling can also help with this problem.

Fetal Alcohol Syndrome (FAS) and Fetal Alcohol Effects (FAE) are common medical problems faced by foster children. They can occur when a mother drinks any alcohol at any time during her pregnancy. There are many web sites devoted to this syndrome, but the most informative one I have found is put out by the National Organization on Fetal Alcohol Syndrome. At the time I viewed it the address was www.nofas.org. This site describes it in great detail. FAS can affect the physical appearance, internal systems and organs, and the mental and emotional state of the child. What type of alcohol and when it was consumed determine what problems may occur. The problems that result from FAS and FAE do not go away. Many can be treated, but few can be cured. New problems may develop throughout the child's life. FAS and FAE are nearly identical problems. The only difference between the two is that FAE does not commonly have physical symptoms. There are prominent facial features used to diagnose FAS, but a neurologist is required to obtain a definitive diagnosis. The facial features that are most common are widely spaced eyes and a flat bridge to the nose. There is usually no indention between the nose and upper lip and the child often has a high forehead and a smaller head.

There are a growing number of babies and young children coming into foster care who are generalized as "meth babies". The use of methamphetamine (meth) is growing in the United States. The children of "meth" users are suffering. The children who are exposed to "meth" may have problems with organs, skin and the nervous system. A parent on "meth" is often not aware of their children's needs so the children are often neglected as well. Because of this growing problem, a lot of web sites are devoted to informing the public about methamphetamine use and its dangers.

Reactive Attachment Disorder (RAD) is another common problem. This is a mental disorder that affects the social skills of the child. They are unable to attach to anyone because of past experiences in their lives. RAD can be caused by neglect and abuse and by frequent changes in the child's life among other causes. Each of these causes is common for foster children and many foster children suffer from RAD. A child with RAD needs more structure and therapy to overcome this disorder. A child with RAD will also be very manipulative. It is a very difficult challenge for a foster parent to handle.

Another challenge that is very obvious yet needs to be mentioned is the lack of life skills a foster child may have. As before mentioned, a child who comes into care may not have even the most basic of life skills such as basic hygiene, communication, etc. Many of these children have never been taught how to brush their teeth or use a fork. These are basic skills that we take for granted, but remember the kind of lives they have lived and be prepared to spend a lot of time teaching these skills. A child who has been moved from foster home to foster home may also lack these skills. Each foster home may assume the child knows these skills and never bothers to teach the child. They may need to be taught how to socialize. Older children need additional skills such as balancing a checkbook and applying for a job. Take the time to teach these basics so that the child does not leave your home as lost as when they came.

> *Be prepared to spend a lot of time teaching basic life skills.*

Foster children have often been exposed to more situations than your own children and at a much younger age. It is upsetting when a three year old child knows about drugs and gangs.

Remember, these children have been taught adult things from infancy; it can take a long time to retrain the child. Patience and consistency are the best defense against these behaviors. You may have to be very strict when the child first enters your home and then relax the rules as they learn to self discipline and to control their own behaviors. Humor can also be used to diffuse a rough situation, especially with older children. If you cannot learn to laugh at a situation, the foster child will cause you a lot of stress. They have learned to work the system and can push you further than your own children might.

Religion can be a big challenge to overcome. With so many diverse religions, it is unlikely that your foster child will share your religion. Some biological parents do not care which religion their children practice, but others may be very concerned. The state allows you to take a foster child with you to church and religious activities, but use good judgement. If something may be perceived as controversial, ask permission first. Baptism is a controversial topic. Always consult with the caseworker before a child is baptized.

Other challenges relate to the holidays and how they are celebrated. Family and religious traditions vary for most holidays. The children in your care will not be used to your traditions. This can cause conflict as you enter the holiday season. It may be that you, or the foster child, celebrate other religious holidays. The child's biological family may prefer you celebrate in the way they are accustomed to. If at all possible, their wishes should be granted. In some cases, it may not be possible or desirable to celebrate in the way the child is accustomed. If a conflict arises, you, the child, the caseworker and possibly the child's biological family will need to come to an agreement on this matter.

Another holiday challenge is visitation. The biological family may wish to visit the child on or near certain holidays and birthdays. This could conflict with your own travel plans and celebration plans for the holidays. Try to be open-minded about such visits and a solution shouldn't be difficult to achieve. The caseworker will help you arrive at a workable solution. Notify the caseworker as early as possible about any travel plans or conflicting celebrations, to minimize conflict.

Foster children have been through a lot in their short lives so foster parenting is often more challenging and more time consuming than parenting a biological child. They often require more constant supervision and care. The children who have been in the system for several years may have learned how to "work the system." They have learned how to be more manipulative and how to pit caseworkers against foster parents. You must have a greater awareness of the problems and challenges in order to overcome them. But, the challenges can be overcome because children are resilient, and when they are overcome, the rewards will be great.

Chapter Ten

What are the Major Financial Concerns

Many of the myths surrounding foster parenting concern money. There are both positive and negative comments made. Most of the negative comments are reinforced by television's depiction of foster homes. Some of the negative comments I have heard are: "Foster parents are only in it for the money." and "Only poor people are foster parents." On the other hand a nurse, after learning I was a foster parent, said "I thought you had to be rich to be a foster parent." So which comment is most accurate? My answer is "All of them" and "none of them". The truth is there are many types of foster parents. Some have money to spare, some do not, and unfortunately yes, some are just "in it for the money."

It isn't important whether or not you have money, but do not underestimate the importance of the financial aspects of foster parenting. So, how much do foster parents get paid? The answer is NOTHING! Foster parents may get a reimbursement, but this is different than getting paid. In Texas, foster parents are given a set amount of reimbursement. This amount varies according to the level of the child. A greater reimbursement is paid for children at higher levels. I asked a foster mom whether the higher reimbursement was really needed. She said yes and went on to describe the extra expenses involved. Her answer was "My children with higher levels destroy everything around them. They do monetarily cost more than the state could supply. They require expensive security monitoring systems. They require their own bedrooms. They also require all of your time and energy. Not to mention all of the ener-

What are the Major Financial Concerns

gy and money you have to spend on literature trying to figure out how to handle their behaviors." You may not have all of these expenses, but any child could potentially require them.

For more information on the levels of foster children, read Chapter 2: What to Do First. The reimbursement amount changes periodically so I will not list specific dollar values here. Each state has its own set of rules for reimbursements. Some states allow each county to determine their own rates and some states do not pay any reimbursements. Others may require you to keep track of the money spent on the child to determine a reimbursement. For exact values, check out your state web page. It should have the most accurate and up-to-date information. A list of these state web pages is provided in the appendix.

This reimbursement is the reason many believe foster parents are just in it for the money. In some cases, this is true. Some people become foster parents to make money; however, if you "do it right" and provide for the kids as you would your own children, this is not the case. The reimbursement will help with the cost associated with raising a child, but it will not cover all expenses such as furniture, clothing, food, transportation, etc. If your only reason for becoming a foster parent is to make money, please reconsider your decision. There are plenty of jobs available to do that that will not cause more harm to the children in foster care. These children deserve all that you can give them, not just financially, but also of your time and of your love.

A clothing allowance is provided in some areas. This is a small amount of money given at set times throughout the child's stay in care. This amount, if any exists, varies tremendously. Even if your county offers it currently, they may discontinue it if their budget is reduced. This is generally a small amount designed to cover the cost of basic and minimal clothing. Sometimes it is a set amount and other times it is only furnished after receipts from purchases are turned in. It may be given when the child is initially placed with you, at changes in seasons, at Christmas time, or at any other time determined by the county. The determining county is the county that the child is from, not necessarily the county you reside in. If you have several children in your care that were placed from different counties, they may not all receive the same amount. You may or may not ever receive this amount even if you are promised it, so do not depend on it. We have had children from three different counties. We were promised a clothing allowance at the time of placement for some of our children. At a later date, the caseworker mentioned that we would be getting another clothing allowance. We told her we had never received the initial one. She promised to have it sent, but to date we have never received a clothing allowance on any of the children in our care. Some areas also provide birthday or Christmas allowances. We have received birthday allowances on some of our children.

Christmas is another time when financial decisions must be made. Some of our children's names were placed on a giving tree by the local CASA. These children received some gifts of toys and clothing from donations to the giving tree. The other children in our care did not receive these gifts. If you don't plan for something like this, you may have one child receiving quite a few more gifts than the others. The gifts received from these types of donations may also vary considerably. Imagine how a child in your care would feel if their foster sibling received several more toys and clothing items for Christmas than they received. We as adults understand the cause of this, but the children may not. Even if they understand, they will still likely feel hurt and cheated. The gifts are often given to you, the parent, to distribute to the child. This has been the case with us. We have several children close in age so we just divided the toys up. Our children were also very young and did not notice the gifts much. You will need to decide ahead of time what works best for your family.

Sometimes the child's parents may give their child a gift. Do not withhold the child's gift from them. Think about how you will handle this and how you can prepare the children in your care for this possibility. You will also need to decide how much, if any, of your own money you will spend on the children. It is your money so this is not a decision I can make for you, but please consider how the children in your care will feel if they do not receive any gifts or if the gifts are unequally distributed. The same is true if you have biological children in your home. Will they be receiving an equal distribution of gifts? What if you receive a placement right before the holiday? Do you have a plan for them?

What if you do not celebrate Christmas? That is okay too, but the same decisions will still apply to you. If a child receives outside gifts, how will you handle this? If a parent gives a child in your care a gift, you cannot withhold it from them. Remember, some of the children in your care may be expecting gifts. If you do not celebrate the holidays, you will need to prepare the children for this. Let the child know what to expect at your house during the holidays.

Another financial consideration is birthdays. Will you throw a party for the child? Will there be gifts, a cake, etc.? These items all cost money. You need to have a plan for handling this occasion as well. Halloween is another holiday with expenses. Will you purchase or make costumes for the children? Will they participate in any parties that may require you to provide something for the child? What about Valentine's Day, Easter, and all other holidays?

Vacations are another expense that should be considered. Think about your usual activities during the year. Will the children in your care accompany you on your vacations? If not, who will care for them while you are gone? How much will that cost you? If they accompany you, factor in the extra costs of larger hotel rooms, more tickets, etc. There are many financial factors to consider when planning for vacations whether the child accompanies you or not.

These are some of the extra expenses you will encounter, but what about the initial expenses and day to day life? Before a child ever comes to live with you, you need to purchase several items. I have provided a list at the end of the book of many of the items necessary before you take in foster children. Some of the more expensive items include furniture such as beds and dressers. These can often be purchased used or perhaps even borrowed from friends. Bedding and clothing are additional expenses. Don't forget toys and toiletries. Although these are somewhat cheaper, they are still expenses that must be factored in. The list provided is much more detailed than what I have mentioned here so check it out before getting started to avoid forgetting an essential item.

A major expense is transportation. Your vehicle must be big enough to transport all of the children you take in. If you are taking in more than three children a car or truck won't be big enough. Most foster parents opt for minivans, SUV's, and full size vans. In addition to the vehicle itself, you must have appropriate car seats for younger children. Don't assume the child will come with one. We have only had one child come with a seat and his was old and in poor condition. CPS can often loan you one for a short time, but it is beneficial to have your own. Many communities have programs that will provide you with a car seat. Many of these programs are offered through law enforcement agencies and hospitals. Your case worker or local foster parent association may be able to provide you with more information for your area.

Once the child is in your home there will be other ongoing expenses as with all children. Your grocery bill will increase, along with any other miscellaneous stores you use. Supplies will run out and need to be replenished, and the children will outgrow or wear out their clothing on a regular basis. Supplies for school and extra curricular activities will be an added expense. Again, some communities may provide help with these expenses, but don't depend on it.

The children have celebrated holidays differently in the past and may have different expectations for them.

In Texas, Medicaid will cover the child's medical expenses and prescriptions. It will not cover the cost of over-the-counter medication such as pain killers, cold medications and vitamins.

What are the Major Financial Concerns

There are other expenses that you may encounter that will be unique to your family or to the child you take in. This section was written to make you aware of many of the possible expenses involved in foster care and not to be used as a comprehensive list. Young foster children also qualify for Women, Infants, and Children (WIC), which will cover the cost of some food items such as milk, formula and cereal. More information can be found concerning this service by contacting WIC directly.

The reimbursement level in Texas is currently sufficient for most expenses you will incur. However, the rates in other states vary considerably. If you are concerned about being able to afford to provide foster care, consult with your local department and plan a budget before you become a foster parent. There are many additional expenses associated with foster care, just as with adding a biological child. With proper planning, most financial concerns can be handled.

Chapter Eleven

What Happens if You are Investigated

Investigations are a foster parent's worst nightmare. No one wants to be investigated as an abusive parent. This is especially true for those of us who spend our time caring for abused and neglected children. However, the longer you are a foster parent, the more likely you are to undergo just such an investigation. We as foster parents, make ourselves targets for allegations just by being who we are. We take in children who may have emotional or behavioral problems and who come from homes where the child has not been properly cared for. Accusations may be made by an angry neighbor, a stranger who disagrees with you, the child's biological parents or the child themselves. Some manipulative older children may use doctors to make the report, by falsely confiding to the doctor about your treatment of them. Day care centers and schools are the most common reporters because they often have the most contact with the children.

There are many reasons for investigations. Many of these reasons are the same that caused the child to enter the foster care system. These reasons may include unsanitary living conditions, poor supervision or neglect, having an unrelated adult in your home, and abuse of any kind. Others are more specific to foster families such as the use of any physical punishment or the child running away from your home. There are several factors that increase the likelihood of you receiving an allegation. These include the length of time you have been fostering, how long a child has been in care, the age of the child, and the physical and emotional, behavioral and medical needs of the child. For example, a teenage foster child who has been in care for many years in many different foster homes, and has some behavioral or emotional problems is more likely to make an allegation against you.

Allegations are made against foster parents in the same way that they are made against anyone else. Someone calls the hotline or informs law enforcement about suspected abuse or neglect. Once an allegation is called in and a report made, the investigation begins. If the child suffers a major injury (or frequent injuries), is suicidal, runs away or is involved in any illegal activity, an investigation will automatically be conducted. When an investigation is begun, an attempt is made to speak with the child involved first. They may be interviewed at school or day care and in this case you will not even know it took place until after the interview. When you are contacted, the initial report will be discussed with you. By law, the investigator cannot tell you who made the report. During the investigation, all children in your home may be interviewed, including any biological or previously adopted children. Anyone else who is accused or who may know something will also be interviewed. The investigator will look into all documents concerning the child, including medical and psychiatric records, that may explain the accusation. For instance, some children may falsely report you because they want to return to their biological home. When a final decision is made, you will receive formal notification and may review the report personally.

If you are being investigated you may wish to hire an attorney at your own expense. They can advise you as to your rights and what actions, if any, you should take. I strongly advise you to hire an attorney as soon as possible. If you have followed my advice for all foster parents, you will already have an attorney selected. Attorneys who specialize in family law will know how to protect you and can help you obtain the best possible outcome for the investigation. The information in the final report will not be publicly disclosed; however, the original accusing party may be allowed to learn the results. Others who may be given copies of the report are the biological parents, future adoptive parents and any courts or attorneys involved. Law enforcement and other officials will be given the report as well. They may take separate action if a criminal act was committed or alleged to have been committed.

The child involved will not automatically be removed from your home, but they may be removed at any time if they are considered to be at risk. When the investigation is concluded, and if corroborated, punitive action will be taken. Your home may be closed temporarily or permanently. The child may be removed from your home temporarily, permanently or not at all. It is also possible that the child will be left in your home, but your home will be closed to all future placements. Once investigated, even if the allegation is found to be unfounded, and your home is left open, you may never receive another placement because the CPU will be aware of the investigation. In fact, there are three possible findings for any investigation: guilty, not guilty or reason to believe. With two out of the three findings, your home will likely be closed.

It may be possible for you to negotiate an appropriate corrective action that is acceptable to all parties involved. Again, this will be easier if you have an attorney representing you. If you disagree with the findings, you may request an administrative review. This review will be conducted at your expense and may not change the findings.

So what can you do to prevent an investigation? One of the best solutions is to study the state guidelines for children in care, otherwise known as the minimum standards, and follow them exactly. Always be truthful with the child's caseworker and with your caseworker or case manager. Have a set of house rules posted and provide it to each child in your care. If they are old enough, have them sign a copy of these rules. Another preventative measure you can take is to know as much as you can about a child before you take them in.

If they are coming from another foster home or have been in the system for a long time, you need to be more informed before you agree to take them. Be sure to ask the questions provided in the appendix before you accept a child from a previous placement. You will also want to know if there have been any investigations in any of the homes where the child has been previously placed. Find out if the child has any behavioral or emotional problems that might make them more susceptible to making an accusation. Make every effort to speak with the foster home the child is coming from to learn any further useful information.

The consequences are high, but if you follow the rules, you will survive an investigation

Be sure to keep your home safe and clean. Do not allow any violations of the state code in your home. Never use physical punishment on any foster child and always provide appropriate supervision of the children. If you notice any unusual behaviors in the child, such as accumulating money, rebellion and talking about running away, notify the caseworker immediately. Follow the plan of service provided to you at the PPT meeting, including attending all requested visits and appointments. Most importantly, use common sense! Most allegations are made because of carelessness on the part of the foster family. When in doubt as to how to handle a particular situation, ask or notify the caseworker, in writing, keeping a copy of the correspondence for yourself. The more proof you can provide countering any allegations made against you, the better off you will be.

Unfortunately, foster parents are held to a higher standard than other parents. We are expected to be better parents and to not make mistakes. The consequences for mistakes are greater for foster parents. We are not always given second chances and contrary to the amendment, we are often considered guilty until proven innocent. Because of these unfair standards, we must be more careful and take every precaution to prevent allegations. Remember, the consequences are high, but if you follow the rules, you will survive an investigation.

Chapter Twelve

How do You Adopt From the System

My family chose to foster because we wanted to adopt children. Like many, we could not afford to pay $15,000, $20,000, $30,000 or possibly much more to adopt a child. We also did not want to be placed on a waiting list indefinitely. We saw foster care as a great alternative. The children in foster care need good homes to go to when they cannot return home or to a relative. We wanted to help some of these children through adoption.

You may be thinking, if we just wanted to adopt, why foster at all? Wouldn't it be easier to just adopt from the state without the risk of losing a child you care for? The answer is "not necessarily". Although it is possible to adopt from the state without fostering first, it is much harder and less likely to occur. The search for adoptive parents begins before a child becomes available for adoption from the state. When it becomes apparent that parental rights will likely be terminated, and there are no acceptable relatives to raise the child, an adoption worker is assigned to the case. This worker begins looking for a possible permanent home for the child. It is seldom beneficial to move a child from home to home; therefore, the first possibility is the current foster home. If the foster parents are certified to adopt or willing to be certified and want to adopt the child, they are often given first priority. If they do not wish to adopt the child, or are not able to, the adoption worker continues the search. They will then search for a foster home that is interested in adopting the child and the child will be moved into this home as soon as possible. They may check with other adoption workers if they are unable to locate a suitable home. Only when no home is found will the child be made available to a family interested only in adoption.

This may sound like discrimination on the part of the state, but it is not. The earlier a child can be moved into its new home, the sooner new attachments can be formed. If a home is certified as a foster and adoptive home, the child can be moved into this new home before the child is legally free for adoption. If the home is only certified to adopt, the child can not be moved until the child is ready to be placed for adoption.

Healthy Caucasian children under age six with no siblings are the easiest to find adoptive placements for and seldom require an extensive search for an adoptive home. Children who have medical disabilities, are of a minority race, are older than age six, or who are a part of a sibling group are harder to place. If you desire to adopt one of these "harder to place" children, it may be possible to adopt without first fostering. It is possible to adopt a relatively easy placement without fostering, but you need to understand that it may take a while before one becomes available.

In my local foster parent association, I have encountered some prospective adoptive families. One such family had been certified as an adoptive home and had been waiting for two years with no success. They decided to become a foster/adopt home and received placements very quickly. They did not necessarily get to adopt these first placements, but their odds of adopting increased greatly with this change in status.

Another option available for foster parents is known as "legal risk". This is the name of the process that involves placing a child with you for adoption, from another foster home. These placements are of children that are legally free for adoption or are likely to be adoptable soon, and are being moved into a home that will hopefully become a permanent home. It may still be considered a foster placement for a short time before the adoptive placement occurs. One of our placements fell into this category. If you are interested in accepting a "legal risk" child, you should notify the adoption worker for your area at the time you become a foster parent. They will then be aware of you when they begin searching for a home for a child. The risk of losing a child in your care is less when you accept placements in this manner. It is not however, risk free. A child is not yours until the adoption is finalized and not even then in rare cases. If you are involved in one of these rare cases, you will know before the adoption occurs. I only put this warning here to make you aware that it can occur. Your adoption worker can always explain this to you further if you need.

We chose to foster first and in just over a year, we had completed our first adoption through the foster care system. This child had been our second foster placement. I have known several other foster parents who have had similar success with adoptions through the state system. In our training class, we were told that adoption of foster children is very rare and that none of us should expect it to happen for a long time, if at all. This may be and possibly is true for some areas, but from personal experience, I have not found this to be the case. In just under three years as foster parents, we adopted four children. Even though we were able to adopt quickly, the process was and is not without its challenges.

I think personal experience is the best teacher so I am going to relate our experiences with adoptions, as well as those from other foster parents, for you to learn from. I will first give you some basic information common to most adoptions and later describe some extreme cases that we have encountered. This should give you some idea of what to expect when you adopt from the state.

Before a child can be placed for adoption, there are a few tasks that must be done. If the child is a foster child in your home, these tasks are your responsibility. If the child is not in your home, these tasks will be completed prior to the placement. The child must have a physical exam, signed by a doctor, within 30 days of placement if they are 23 months or younger, or within 3 months if they are 24 months or older. They must have a current dental exam. The child must have a current Tuberculosis test referred to as a PPD or a TB skin test. This test is performed by the physician.

How do You Adopt From the System

Any child older than six months will "discuss" adoption with their worker three times. A child under six months must have one discussion. This is appropriate for older children, but seems quite foolish for infants and toddlers who generally have no idea what is happening to them. The workers often mention how foolish they feel when conducting these "discussions" with very young children.

Counseling is provided to all children two years and older. The mental, emotional and developmental status is assessed by a doctor or other professional in contact with the child. This must also be done within 30 days of placement for children 18 months and younger, within 3 months for 18 month to five years old and within six months for children older than 5 years.

When a child is placed for adoption, they are no longer considered a foster child. If they were already in your home, the adoption worker will come to your home to officially place the child for adoption. If they were not previously in your home, they will be brought to you and the placement will begin. The placement itself involves more paperwork. This paperwork is similar to that which you are provided with when a child is placed in foster care. You will sign a "Designation of Medical Consenter for Non-DFPS Employee" form which allows you to provide care for the child. This form explains all procedures which must be followed for medical treatment and testing. There is also an "Informed Consent" form for the primary designee for medical care that explains how to receive informed consent for medical care. There is an "Adoptive Placement Agreement" form which explains your responsibilities and those of the Department of Family Protective Services (DFPS). The "Discipline Notification" form must also be completed at this time. This form describes the discipline used in your home and the approved methods of discipline. You will be asked to sign two copies of each of these forms, one for DFPS and one for yourself. These forms differ very little from the forms signed when a child is placed in foster care. The main difference in these forms is the child's name. The forms are filled out with the name you will give the child when adopted, not their birth name.

You will also be given a copy of the Health, Social, Educational, and Genetic History (HSEGH, pronounced hessig) report. This report must have been completed within the last three months. You must initial each page of the report and sign at the end stating that you have been given this report. This report is very important to you. Be sure to read it carefully. It contains all known information on the child's family history. It contains information on the birth parents, any siblings, grandparents, and any other close relatives. It will hopefully provide you with health information as well as other pertinent information on the child's birth family; however, it may lack crucial information if DFPS has been unable to acquire that information. This form will help you to know where the child came from and what problems you may expect in the future. This form will explain the circumstances for the removal of the child from the birth parents and the reasons this child cannot be placed with any relatives. If you were the foster parent for this child, you will already know some of this information and may have even assisted in providing some of the information for this report. It is still important that you read this report carefully, because it is unlikely that you know everything.

In addition to this report, you will receive the entire redacted DFPS case file for the child. The term "redacted case file" simply means that all information concerning private information on the prior placements or of the parents has been removed from the file. Even without this information, it is a very extensive and valuable file. This file contains every detail of the child's case from the moment the case began. This is an extensive amount of paperwork. Every invitation to a PPT meeting or court notice to each recipient is copied into this file. Every medical visit, the Service Plan, and any other correspondence will be in this file. One of the files we received contained an approximately two-inch thick stack of paper. This was a small file. We have also received one that contained three, three-inch thick binders of paper. Obviously this paperwork will take a while to look through, but you should try to at least scan as much of it as possible. It may contain important details concerning the case, the child, or the child's family that you may want to know before you adopt the child. This information can also be used to explain why the child was adopted when they are old enough to understand. If a picture of the birth parents is not included in the file, you may wish to ask for one. Depending upon the particular case, it may or may not be possible to obtain one at this point. Having a picture of the birth parents may help the child with their adjustment to your family, or later in life when they are curious about their heritage.

After the placement, any questions you have should be directed to the adoption worker not the caseworker. In some cases, there may still be a need to contact the caseworker so do not discard their name and contact information just because a new worker has been assigned. Depending on the circumstances surrounding the adoption placement, the original caseworker may still be involved in the child's case. The involvement of the previous worker can occur in situations ranging from an unresolved issue relating to the case to simply the adoption worker being on vacation.

In the case of two of our adoptions, the adoption worker was out on medical leave for an extensive amount of time and the adoptive placement was actually performed by our family's caseworker. Some areas do not have adoption workers and must also rely on others to complete the placement. In these cases, it is crucial that you know what is necessary for the placement to occur so that no steps are forgotten that will delay the placement.

Now that the child has been placed with you, you are not simply in a waiting period. There are things you must still do. A child in foster care, in the state of Texas, is automatically enrolled in Medicaid. This coverage is not guaranteed after the child is placed for adoption. The child must qualify for it as a member of your family to continue coverage in most cases. If you will need this coverage for the child, you must apply for it as soon as possible. The child will only continue to automatically receive this coverage for one month after the placement has occurred. If you will not be using Medicaid, you must place the child on your own insurance.

This is best done prior to losing the current coverage. The child's Medicaid coverage will automatically continue if the child qualifies for it as part of the adoption subsidy.

Adoption subsidy is money paid to a home to assist in covering the costs of raising a child. This subsidy is granted to children who do not fit into the "easy to adopt" category. This subsidy helps some families to adopt a child despite financial difficulties. The children who qualify may be part of a large sibling group being adopted together, a minority race, a medically fragile or needy child, or an older child, or have some other special circumstance. The subsidy is not just for Medicaid coverage and may not include that option at all. It can be a set fee to be paid to the family every month until the child is 18 or until the subsidy is no longer needed. It may be a one-time reimbursement to cover initial costs of placement and adoption. The subsidy may include other special benefits for the child or family. In some cases the attorney's fees, up to a certain dollar amount, may be reimbursed. If a child, in Texas, qualifies for adoption subsidy of any kind, they will also receive a tuition waiver when they attend college.

Adoption subsidy is not automatically granted either. You must apply to receive it. The adoption worker should provide you with the necessary forms to file for subsidy. These forms must be filled out and submitted for review prior to the consummation of the adoption. Even if you do not currently need assistance, I advise you to fill these forms out. If the forms are not submitted prior to the adoption, they cannot be submitted at a later date. The forms can be changed at a later date if circumstances change only if they were initially submitted. The child may not initially qualify for subsidy, but problems may develop later in the child's life, that were unknown at the time of adoption. Fill these forms out even if you do not think the child will qualify. Be as thorough as possible when filling out these forms because you do not know what insignificant fact may qualify a child. These forms ask for information on your income and assets, your monthly expenses and any illnesses, problems or special requirements the child has.

How do You Adopt From the System

After these forms are sent off, you will be contacted by yet another state employee regarding them. They will ask you to further explain any vague references and will negotiate the subsidy, if any, the child will receive. Once an agreement is reached, a new form will be provided you, detailing every aspect of the subsidy. This form must again be signed and returned along with any other requested information. Periodically, over the duration of the subsidy, another form will be sent to you verifying that the subsidy is still needed. These forms must be filled out and returned when they are requested.

Keep in mind that even if a child qualifies for subsidy, the amount will not cover the entire expense of raising them. This subsidy is not a method to make money from an adoption and should not be the reason you want or are willing to adopt a child. Whether or not the child qualifies for subsidy, the foster care reimbursements stop when the child is placed for adoption. If the child was in foster care in your home, and you received a monthly reimbursement, be aware that money will not be sent to you as of the date of the placement. The child is not legally yours yet, but you are entirely responsible for the expenses related to caring for the child.

You pay the attorney's bill so it is your right to know the answers to your questions.

Now the wait begins. The child must be in your home for a minimum of six months before an adoption can take place. If you have fostered this child, you may have already met this requirement. If you did not, you must wait the required six months. It is possible for the judge to waive this waiting period, but DFPS is normally against this waiver. The Department of Family and Protective Services wants to ensure that the child fits into the adoptive home before the adoption takes place. This six month period gives both the adoptive parents and the child a chance to "try out" the living arrangement. It is generally a long enough period to know if there is a problem that needs to be, or cannot be,

How do You Adopt From the System

worked out prior to the adoption. Sometimes children just do not adjust well to certain environments and personality clashes may evolve. Other times, the prospective adoptive parents will find that they are not able to handle the child or are not capable of parenting the child. If the match is not healthy, or found to be a good fit for either party, it is better to find out before the adoption takes place. This way the department can find a suitable home and the child does not have to be removed from another "permanent" home at a later date.

    I recommend that you locate an attorney when you first enter foster care, but if you do not already have one, now is the time to hire one. The child's adoption worker may have a list of attorneys that have worked with DFPS before. You do not have to select from this list, but having an attorney who is already familiar with a foster care adoption, may be to your advantage. If you know of another foster family who has undergone an adoption, you may want to consult with them on their choice of attorneys. They may have had a great experience or a terrible one. This information may assist you to find an attorney you will be able to work with. If you do not have a good recommendation from a friend or if you would like more information before you decide; try to contact as many attorneys as you can. Ask each attorney if they have any experience working with adoptions, particularly foster care adoptions, what their area of expertise is, and what their fees are. There are likely to be additional fees with the adoption. Be sure to ask about these fees as well to make sure there are no hidden costs. The attorney should be able to give you an accurate estimate including all additional fees. If they will not do this, find a different attorney. Remember, you will be paying the attorney to help you so it is your right to know the answers to these and any other questions you may have. The fees an attorney charges will vary greatly, even within a particular area. The cheapest may not be the best choice. As with all things, you get what you pay for. That does not mean you should select the most expensive either.

    Some attorneys may require a meeting with you before they will answer your questions, others will not. Some attorneys may require full payment up front; others require only a deposit up front with the remainder due upon conclusion of the case. Be sure to discuss this with the attorney so that problems do not arise later. Many attorneys are willing to work with you in setting up a payment plan for their fees. If you do not feel comfortable with a particular attorney, seek out another. Select the attorney who will best suit your needs.

After the six month waiting period is up, the adoption hearing will take place. Your attorney may already have a court date lined up by this time. If not, one should be arranged at this time. If you are in a city, there might be several possibilities within a reasonable amount of time. The judge will select one for you, but if the date is not acceptable, you may request a different date. If you live in a rural community, you may share a judge with several other communities. This judge may only be in your area one day each month. This was the case for some of our children. If you are not able to make the date set for your case, you will have to wait another month.

The hearing itself is usually not a long hearing. By this time, the parental rights of the birth parents have been terminated and everything should be ready for the adoption to occur. All paperwork and requirements should have been completed. Those in attendance will include: the adoption worker, the DFPS attorney, the child's CASA worker (if they have not already been dismissed), your attorney, the judge, a court reporter (this may be done by another party already included in the hearing), you and your spouse and the child. You are usually allowed to have other family members or guests present at this hearing.

The judge will verify that all paperwork has been completed and that DFPS consents to the adoption. You and your spouse will be asked a series of questions relating to your required tasks and your reasons for wanting to adopt the child. If no one objects, the judge will rule on the adoption. You may wish to bring a camera with you to this hearing to commemorate the event. Your attorney and the DFPS personnel may have theirs as well.

Unlike with traditional adoptions, there are no post-placement studies to be done and the adoption is consummated immediately. Once the child has been adopted, they are your child and DFPS will no longer have any legal control over them. You are now finally free to raise your child without DFPS involvement. Don't forget to have the child's name officially changed for their social security card. If you qualified for subsidy, you will need to mail certified copies of certain court documents to continue the subsidy. The specific list of documents and time frames in which they must be sent, is provided with the notification of subsidy at the time it is granted. There are post-adoption programs available to assist with any issues related to adoption of the child for both you and your child. The adoption worker should have provided you with information concerning how to set up these services prior to the adoption. These services are generally voluntary and are designed to assist you and the child with the adjustment and are not designed to control your parenting of the child.

Chapter Thirteen

Who Else Will Be Involved

There are quite a few people involved with the foster care system. You will meet many of them, but others you may not even hear about. I will introduce everyone involved in a typical case one by one so that you will know who is involved in the child's case and who you may come in contact with.

The first person you will likely meet is the recruiter or trainer of new foster families. This person may also be the Foster/Adoptive Home Development worker (FAD). They are in charge of the orientation meeting and setting up the training classes. They may also be the person who reviews your application and certifies all new foster parents. After you are certified, a FAD will be assigned to your family. This worker may be the same individual that set up your training, but this is not always the case. This worker becomes your case worker or case manager. They are responsible for monitoring each foster home and making sure they are adhering to all regulations. They also act as liaison between the foster family and the agency. You will get to know this person quite well and they can help you throughout the process of foster parenting.

The next people you will likely meet are the trainers. These are the people who provide you with your initial training. There are usually two or more of these trainers at every training class. If you attend the Department of Family and Protective Services' PRIDE training, you will likely receive instruction from one employee of the department and one foster parent (or former foster parent).

Who Else Will Be Involved

These are the preferred trainers, but regions may vary on this. You may remain in contact with your trainers throughout your time as a foster parent. They are usually involved with foster parent associations which are described in Chapter 14: What Resources Are Available.

The person who performs your home study may be a department employee or a contracted individual. The home study requires a lot of work and is time consuming. It is sometimes contracted out to avoid occupying the limited and already often overtaxed personnel of the department.

The Family Investigator is the first person that comes in contact with the child. They investigate any reported cases and visit the homes of all reportedly abused or neglected children. They determine whether a child should be removed or not and perform this act as necessary. They are often the person who delivers the child to your home as well. This may be the only time you meet the investigator. This is not always the case however, as they often have other jobs within the department.

The child's caseworker is the person you will likely see the most often. They take over the child's case from the investigator after the child has been removed from their home. They are responsible for monthly (or sometimes more frequent) visits with you, the foster family, and the foster child. They are responsible for supervising any visits the child has with their biological parents and other relatives. They are also in charge of all paperwork related to the child and seeing that the case is properly handled by all involved parties. They are also responsible for overseeing the biological parent's participation in the plan. They report to a supervisor on a regular basis.

The caseworker supervisor oversees the cases of several caseworkers as well as the caseworkers themselves. They only become directly involved in a case when the worker requests their assistance and when the case transfers from worker to worker. They may temporarily take over the case during this transition period. The caseworker of one of our children was promoted to this role.

She then passed the case onto another caseworker. Later that caseworker left and the supervisor temporarily managed the case again. It is not uncommon for caseworkers to change positions within the department and you will come in contact with caseworkers and their supervisors on a regular basis.

The biological parents are obviously involved with the child's case and you may or may not ever meet them. The biological parents, for those unfamiliar with the term, are the parents that contributed to the birth of the child. I met the biological mothers of three of my four adopted children and the biological father of two of them. One mother I saw only once, the other set of parents I saw on many occasions. If the child comes to you after the parental rights have been terminated, you will probably never meet their biological parents. It is also quite common for there to be an unknown father. The biological mother may not even know who the father was, thus, making it impossible to meet him.

The biological parents are often required to attend parenting classes. There is a parent trainer to conduct these classes. You may see this person on occasion as the child is often a part of the classes. They are an important part of the case, but not someone you will be directly in contact with.

The legal side of the case brings several others into the child's case. DFPS has a legal department that is responsible for preparing for all court appearances on behalf of the department. In smaller regions there may only be one person handling all the cases. You will meet this person any time you attend the court hearings. You may also come into contact with the legal representative if you have legal questions concerning the case. I have found it easier to contact my own attorney and have him contact the legal department. He is more likely to get answers than if I contact them directly.

Each party involved with the case will have an attorney. This person is provided by the court if the parents do not have their own representative. There is a separate attorney provided for the biological mother and the biological father. In many cases, one parent may lose rights to the child while the other retains them so separate legal counsel is required. The child receives their own attorney as well. Occasionally, you will be contacted by the child's attorney for information concerning the child's behavior and condition throughout the case. The other assigned attorneys are not likely to contact you because they are not working for the child in your care. These attorneys are dismissed from the case at the termination of the parental rights or when the child returns home. If an appeal is filed, a new attorney will be assigned. Each party's attorney is assigned from a pool of attorneys. The judge selects and assigns each of these attorneys at the initial hearing. The assigned attorneys are the same attorneys you might hire as your own, so make sure they are not already involved in the case when you hire them.

The judge controls the case from a legal standpoint. He, or she, decides whether the child will remain in care, for how long, and with whom. They are the single most important person involved with the case because all permanent decisions are made by them. You may be asked to testify before the judge during the case, but you will never personally meet them.

The final person involved with the court side of the child's case is a Court Appointed Special Advocate (CASA) worker. In some areas they are called guardians ad litem (GALs). Not all children are assigned CASA workers. When one is available and if the judge feels one is necessary, the judge will appoint a CASA worker for the child. This is a volunteer position and it is this person's job to advocate on behalf of the child. They will contact you periodically throughout the case to obtain any helpful information concerning the child. The volunteer will ask you questions concerning the child's health and behavior and how it has changed since the child's arrival. They will also meet with the child and speak with them when applicable. They conduct their own investigation into the case and provide a written report to the judge before all hearings. The CASA worker is an independent party that is concerned only with the best interest of the child. These workers play a very important role in the child's case because they can advocate directly to the judge through their reports. The CASA worker is usually dismissed when the child returns home or the parental rights are terminated, but they may remain on the case for a longer time period if their services are still considered necessary.

If the parental rights have been terminated and no suitable relative has been found, the adoption worker takes over the case. They are now the child's new caseworker. The adoption worker attempts to find a home for the child. They review home studies of prospective adoptive homes to find a suitable match. The adoption worker has the task of placing the child for adoption in either the home the child currently resides in or in whatever suitable home they have found. The worker is now responsible for all paperwork and monthly visits until the adoption is consummated.

If you are planning to adopt, you will also be in contact with the adoption subsidy negotiator. This person determines how much subsidy, if any, the child will receive after the adoption. One person often performs this role for several regions. Because of this, unless you reside near their office, you will only speak with this person on the phone or through mail or email. This is one of the last people you will come in contact with in the system.

All of these people play an important role in the child's case. These are not the only people you may encounter. In fact, there are several others who are not directly involved with the case that you may meet and utilize their services. I have described several of these others in Chapter 14: What Resources Are Available. The people and positions described provide an overview of all those involved in the child's case and should give an idea of how many people are involved with a single case.

Chapter Fourteen

What Resources are Available

There are many resources available to foster parents. Knowing where to look or whom to ask can be helpful. Resources are available for both personal and professional use and provide a wide variety of assistance. In this chapter, I will mention several of the more common ones. Some may be very obvious to you, but others are often overlooked. The more resources at your disposal, the better prepared you will be, so become aware of as many resources as possible before you need them.

One of the most obvious resources is family. If your family supports your decision to foster, and sometimes even when they don't, they can assist you in many ways. Families often provide emotional support. This can be very helpful whether you are anxious, worried, angry, elated or depressed. They may also be able to help with financial needs or with collecting necessary supplies. They may be able to provide hand-me-down clothing or furniture when you need it quickly, or even assist with day-to-day activities. Regardless of their role they can be a valuable asset.

Friends can assist in many or even all of the ways your family can. Often they live closer to you and may be of even more benefit at times than family can be. Both friends and family are important resources.

Other foster families can assist in many of the same ways as friends and family. They may have additional clothing, supplies or furniture they are not currently using and may be willing to loan these to you. In addition to this, they may know of additional resources that can be very helpful. Other foster families are often facing, or have faced similar challenges to what you will experience. They can offer informed advice based on their own experiences to better help you. Foster parents are able to support you in other ways as well. They understand what you are going through on a deeper emotional level, having experienced the same situations themselves. It is helpful for foster parents to discuss their experiences and emotions with other foster parents.

Many cities have Foster Parent Associations (FPA) for this purpose and to offer training opportunities. These associations have regular meetings. Your caseworker or case manager should be aware of the nearest association. Another resource for locating these associations in Texas is the Texas Foster Family Association (TFFA). This organization provides a lot of information to foster families in Texas. They operate a website that lists the representatives for each region. Their website can be located at www.tffa.org. They also provide a newsletter for their membership. Some local associations provide free membership with TFFA for their local association members. If not, I strongly recommend joining TFFA. They provide information on any local news as well as any legislation currently being developed that will affect fostering. They also provide listings of other useful resources on their website and have an annual conference that is a great way to receive many of your required training hours as a foster parent. Most states have a similar state association. A list of state associations can be found at www.fosterparents.com.

Churches can be another excellent resource for foster parents. If you have a religious affiliation, your own congregation can be very helpful. Often times you can find others willing to loan or give you many of the items such as furniture and clothing you need. Many churches have benevolence rooms where they keep supplies to give to the needy. You may be able to make use of some of these items. Church members can also be a source of emotional support. Many will be willing to listen to your problems and offer support or advice as needed. Many religious organizations also provide counseling services that can be of great use to you as a foster parent.

Whatever your religious affiliation, don't overlook it as a good resource.

Medical professionals are available to help you answer any medical questions you encounter. If you don't already know a good pediatrician, you should locate one before becoming a foster parent. The phone book is a good place to start, but word of mouth is a better alternative. Talk to others whom you know who have children and ask them for recommendations for a good pediatrician. Set up a consultation with any doctor you are considering so that you may meet them before you need their services. Be sure they take Medicaid or whichever insurance you use so that you will not be surprised later. A pediatrician should be able to answer or assist you in finding the answers to your medical questions. If they do not know the answer, they can refer you to a specialist who may. Doctors often have brochures and other information to help with any specific concerns about medical conditions.

Your own medical doctor is also a resource for you. You may be under a lot of stress when you begin to add children to your home. Your doctor can help you cope with this stress. They can also assist you in locating specific information you need and even help you locate a pediatrician. Many people use their own doctors for their children as well. This can be fine as long as your doctor is familiar with and used to working with children. I prefer to use a pediatrician believing children are not just little adults. A pediatrician will more readily recognize symptoms for childhood illnesses and know what illnesses are currently traveling through the children in your community. Remember a pediatrician is a specialist whose specialty is children.

Medicaid is medical insurance provided for families in Texas who can not afford insurance. Foster children automatically qualify for this insurance. Other states have similar plans available, check with your caseworker for more information. Medicaid completely covers all the child's health care needs. It pays 100% of all the child's sick or well-child visits to the doctor, including specialists. It covers dental and eye exams as well. Not all doctors accept Medicaid so again, you will need to ask before taking the child for a visit. Check out Chapter 9: What Are the Greatest Challenges for more information on Medicaid.

The Special Supplemental Nutrition Program for Women, Infants and Children (WIC) is another available resource for foster parents. All foster children under age five are eligible for WIC. If you want this service, you must apply for it at your local state health department or similar agency. WIC provides checks or vouchers to purchase certain foods each month such as milk, formula, cereal and other nutrient-rich foods. A complete listing of these foods is available when you apply for WIC services.

Another great resource is your local school. Schools are able to provide you with resources beyond the classroom. Schools are capable of testing children for learning disabilities such as dyslexia and other reading problems. They also have services for working with a child who has a mental or physical handicap. Depending on the particular handicap, there are many options available for the school. Some students may be assigned a special helper who attends classes with the student to help them when necessary. Other students may be placed in a special class designed to assist them with their handicap. Schools also have other information and resources they can provide you with to assist you at home with the child. Financial assistance is also available from schools. Foster children automatically qualify for free lunch and breakfast if available. When you enroll the child for school you will be given information on this program. If not, ask for it, it can be a valuable resource if you need it.

Your child's teacher is also available to assist you. If you feel the child needs assistance and is being overlooked, contact their teacher and ask them about these services. Their teacher spends a lot of time with them and may already be aware of the particular problem. They may also be able to suggest ways to resolve this problem without additional services. Set up a conference with the child's teacher any time you have a concern. It helps to work with the teacher so that you do not contradict each other's work and confuse the child.

For children under age three, Early Childhood Intervention

What Resources are Available

(ECI) is available. ECI provides many of the same services provided by the school. The state of Texas requires that all foster children be evaluated by ECI upon entering the system. They will evaluate each child and determine which services are needed. The services available include nutrition, physical or occupational therapy, speech therapy, counseling, audiology, vision services and family education among others. Each needed specialist will be scheduled to visit the child in your home for therapy. They will also teach you what to do to further the child's training on a daily basis. Your local school can assist you in contacting your local ECI. Your local ECI or similar services can also be located by calling the DARS inquiry line at 1-800-628-5115. The Department of Assistive and Rehabilitative Services (DARS) is located in Texas, but can direct you to the appropriate resources nationwide for all children under age three.

When seeking out assistance for foster children and foster care, don't overlook the obvious, the Department of Family and Protective Services (DFPS) This department is specifically designed for foster children and foster parents and can offer a variety of services to assist you. Many DFPS offices have a room or closet with donated clothing for use by foster families. When a child comes into care with little or no clothing, they are often given some things from this room. They may also have items such as diaper bags, bottles, diapers, and other items that are necessary immediately upon placement. DFPS also has many brochures and information concerning commonly encountered problems with the children and with foster care in general. If you need anything specific, ask your caseworker or case manager for this information. Your caseworker and the child's caseworker may be able to locate information for you as well. If you are unsure about anything concerning the child, ask the worker. They are often in touch with the biological parents and can obtain important medical information concerning the family. DFPS also has resource lists available for your use. These lists include names of attorneys and medical specialists such as neurologists and psychol-

Be prepared to pay for all professional services

What Resources are Available

ogists. They can also help you locate your local foster parent association and churches with available resources.

Having a personal attorney can be beneficial in numerous ways. When selecting an attorney be sure to select one who specializes in adoptions. One who has worked with the Department of Family and Protective Services before is an even better asset. An attorney already familiar with DFPS will also be familiar with the process of state adoptions. State adoptions vary from agency adoptions in some ways so not all attorneys will understand the different process. Having an attorney can be helpful even if you do not plan to adopt. Our attorney was able to check on the status of a particular child in our care and assisted in moving her case along when it was otherwise stalled. They can work with the DFPS legal department to develop a working strategy for the child's case. Remember, as with any other time you are hiring an attorney, they will expect to be paid for their time and effort. Our attorney billed additional expenses at the time of the adoption, but some will want to be paid as they perform the work for you. You need to arrange any details regarding additional services and their fees with your attorney.

Anyone you encounter, has the potential to be a resource for you.

Many written resources are available for you as a foster parent. There are many books written on adoption, parenting, foster care and on various medical disorders. Each of these may contain specific information for your situation. Several magazines also exist on these topics. *Fostering Families TODAY* is a magazine designed specifically for foster parenting. I recommend reading several books and magazines on pertinent topics so that you will be better prepared to handle whatever comes your way.

I have briefly described several resources available for you as a foster parent. Remember, anyone you encounter, both professionally or personally, has the potential to be a resource for you. Don't overlook anyone in your search for resources to make you a better foster parent.

Chapter Fifteen

How Will It End

The information provided in this book is designed to provide you with some answers to your basic questions on foster parenting, and to provide you with an idea of where to go next. I hope it has made you consider how foster care can affect your life and opened your mind to the possibility of becoming a foster parent.

All rules and procedures in this book are for Texas. The procedures may be similar for other states, but there will be differences. Each state has its own system of rules and it is best to check with your local human services department for the rules governing foster care and adoption in your state. This book is designed to provide you with a simple guide to the state system. But there is one constant to all state systems: the children. Remember, the information in this book is accurate to the best of my knowledge, at the time of its printing, but rules change frequently and you should always consult with your local department for current procedures.

Consult with your local department of child protective services for the most current rules.

Foster parenting is not easy and is often full of challenges, but it offers its share of joy and excitement as well. The amount of information may seem overwhelming at first, but quickly becomes second nature to the foster parent. After reading this book, you may be ready to try it out yourself and become a foster parent. If this is the case, don't hesitate to contact your local Department of Family and Protective Services or a private agency in your area. There are many children in the system needing a loving home and many others who cannot enter the system because there is no home available to accept them. The sooner you become a foster parent, the sooner you can take in one or several of these waiting children.

If being a foster parent is too much or if you are still unsure, you can become certified to provide respite care. Respite care is relief care provided for more than 72 hours. If you choose to provide respite care you must fill out an application and submit to a criminal history check. You must also become certified in CPR and first aid. The requirements for the number of children in your care are the same as for foster parents. In other words, you may still only have a maximum of six children at a time. Overall, the requirements are not as difficult as those for foster care because of the type of care you would provide. This makes respite care a great way to get a taste of what foster care is all about without the same level of commitment.

If after reading this book, you have decided that being a foster parent is definitely not for you, then please think about other ways you can help these children. You may have the resources to donate clothing, supplies or services to foster families. Or you may choose to volunteer for an organization such as CASA. Perhaps you know of someone else who would make a great foster parent that you can share this information with. Whatever your choice, I hope you are at the least better informed about the foster care system and those involved with it.

My family was interviewed for an adoption story presented by a local news station. My biological son was given the opportunity to explain adoption to his class at school following this story. His teacher opened the discussion by saying that he was now sharing his parents with children that were not born into his family. She told him it was a very selfless thing to do. The response my then six year old son gave his teacher amazed her and brought tears to her eyes. He said simply, "In the Bible, it says that if we give, we will receive even more." He went on to tell of his love for his brother and sisters. During the television interview, he had also stated that he wanted another brother. This response from my son should remind all of us that giving of ourselves to these children, is the least of what we can do, and that even a small child can learn from and enjoy what foster care and adoption have to offer.

I, myself, often think of how foster care changed my life. We wanted a larger family and in a few short years, we accomplished just that. We went from a family of three to a family of seven when we adopted four children through the foster care system. For my family, foster care provided us the opportunity to take in a few children and give them the chance at a better life and to improve our lives at the same time. My adopted son recently made the comment "We live in a fixed home." He was referring to the physical house we were working on, but this statement applies to foster homes as well. We constantly hear about broken homes today. Foster parenting is part of the solution to this problem. We are in the business of fixing homes. I have chosen to adopt my son's simple statement as a description of my family and say that "we are a fixed home".

> *The risks are great, but the rewards are greater.*

Each foster family's story is different, but there is one constant in all of them: children's lives are changed. You now have the opportunity to change the lives of children and create your own story. Remember, as you consider becoming a foster parent, the risks are great, but the rewards are greater.

Appendix A

Supply Checklist

- ☐ Beds / crib
- ☐ Sheets
- ☐ Pillows with cases
- ☐ Clothing including socks, underwear and shoes
  (at least one day of clothing for each size of children you are willing to take)
- ☐ Diapers in each size *(if accepting children under age 4)*
- ☐ Baby wipes
- ☐ Formula *(if accepting infants)*
- ☐ Bottles or sippy cups *(if accepting infants or young children)*
- ☐ Baby food *(if accepting infants)*
- ☐ Toothbrushes
- ☐ Children's toothpaste
- ☐ Shampoo
- ☐ Soap
- ☐ Deodorant *(if accepting older children)*
- ☐ Anti-lice shampoo
- ☐ Camera *(for taking pictures of the child and their clothing when they arrive)*
- ☐ Car Seat / booster seat *(if accepting children under age 8)*

Appendix B

Questions to Keep Near Your Phone

1) How old is the child?

2) Is the child male or female?

3) What race is the child?

4) What is the child's name?

5) Why was the child picked up?

6) What medical conditions does the child have?

7) Is the child on any medication?

8) Does the child have any known allergies?

9) Is the child potty trained?

10) How long is the child expected to be in care?

Appendix C

Abuse Hotlines and State Websites

Alabama
1-334-242-9500
www.dhr.state.al.us

Arizona
1-888-767-2445
www.az.gov

California
1-800-540-4000
www.state.ca.us/HomeFamily.html

Connecticut
1-800-842-2288
www.ct.gov/dcf

Florida
1-800-962-2873
www.state.fl.us/cf_web

Hawaii
1-808-832-5300
www.hawaii.gov/dhs

Illinois
1-800-252-2873
www.state.il.us/dcfs

Alaska
1-800-478-4444
www.hss.state.ak.us/ocs

Arkansas
1-800-482-5964
www.arkansas.gov/dhhs

Colorado
local human service
www.cdhs.state.co.us

Delaware
1-800-292-9582
www.dhss.delaware.gov

Georgia
local social services
www.dfcs.dhr.grorgia.gov

Idaho
1-800-422-4453
www.state.id.us/health_safety

Indiana
1-800-800-5556
www.state.in.us/dcs

Iowa
1-800-362-2178
www.dhs.state.ia.us

Kentucky
1-800-752-6200
www.chfs.ky.gov/dcbs

Maine
1-800-452-1999
www.maine.gov/portal/family

Massachusetts
1-800-792-5200
www.mass.gov

Minnesota
local social services
www.dhs.state.mn.us

Missouri
1-800-392-3738
www.dss.mo.gov

Nebraska
1-800-652-1999
www.hhs.state.ne.us

New Hampshire
1-800-894-5533
www.dhhs.nh.gov

New Mexico
1-800-797-3260
www.hsd.state.nm.us

North Carolina
local social services
www.ncdhhs.gov/dss

Kansas
1-800-922-5330
www.kansas.gov

Louisiana
local human services
www.dss.louisiana.gov

Maryland
local social services
www.dhr.state.md.us

Michigan
1-800-942-4357
www.michigan.gov/dhs

Mississippi
1-800-222-8000
www.mdhs.state.ms.us

Montana
1-866-820-5437
www.dphhs.mt.gov

Nevada
1-800-992-5757
www.dcfs.state.nv.us

New Jersey
1-877-652-2873
www.state.nj.us/dcf

New York
1-800-342-3720
www.ocfs.state.ny.us

North Dakota
local social services
www.nd.gov/humanservices

Appendix C - Abuse Hotlines and State Websites

Ohio
local social services
www.jfs.ohio.gov

Oregon
local social services
www.oregon.gov/dhs

Rhode Island
1-800-742-4453
www.dcyf.ri.gov

South Dakota
local social services
www.dss.sd.gov

Texas
1-800-252-5400
www.dfps.state.tx.us

Vermont
local social services
www.dcf.stste.vt.us/fsd

Washington
1-866-363-4276
www.dshs.wa.gov

Wisconsin
local social services
www.dhfs.wisconsin.gov

Oklahoma
1-800-522-3511
www.okdhs.org

Pennsylvania
1-800-932-0313
www.dpw.state.pa.us

South Carolina
local social services
www.state.sc.us/dss

Tennessee
1-877-542-2873
www.tennessee.gov/youth

Utah
1-800-678-9399
www.dhs.utah.gov

Virginia
1-800-552-7096
www.dss.state.va.us

West Virginia
1-800-352-6513
www.wvdhhr.org

Wyoming
local social services
www.dfsweb.state.wy.us

Glossary of Terms and Acronyms

Adoption — The process of legally assuming all responsibilities and parental rights of a child.

Adoption Subsidy — The partial reimbursement for the care of an eligible child adopted from the state system.

Adoptive Home — An individual home that is certified to adopt children.

Adoptive Placement — Placing a child in the home of an adoptive parent pending the child's adoption.

Aging Out — When a foster child turns 18 and graduates from high school and is no longer considered as being in foster care. If they haven't graduated high school, they may remain in care until age 22.

Appeal — Requesting a review of a court case by a higher court.

ARD — Admission, Review and Dismissal. A team put together of educators, and other concerned individuals that evaluates a child and determines what assistance, if any, is needed for their education.

Basic Care Home — A foster home that cares for only basic care or minimal care children.

Glossary of Terms and Acronyms

Biological Family — A family related by blood. The family the child was born into. Also known as the birth family.

CASA — Court Appointed Special Advocate. A person appointed by the court to advocate to the judge on behalf of the foster child.

Case File — All paperwork related to the child and their case created or received by the state agency.

Caseworker — A state or agency employee who is in charge of overseeing the case of the foster child.

Child Abuse — Harm to a child through physical, emotional or sexual abuse.

Court of Appeals — The court that hears and decides on an appeal from a lower court.

CPS — Child Protective Services. A department within the Human Services Department charged with the welfare of children.

CPU — Central Placement Unit. The unit responsible for finding a foster placement for each child.

DARS — Department of Assistive and Rehabilitative Services. The state agency that provides resources for families of children with disabilities and delays.

DFPS — Department of Family and Protective Services. The state department in charge of all family and children welfare matters, including foster care and adoption. This department is a branch of the Human Services Department.

DHS — Department of Human Services. The state department charged with the protection of all children within the state.

Glossary of Terms and Acronyms

ECI — Early Childhood Intervention. A state agency that assists families of children under age three with disabilities and delays.

Emotional Abuse — Any act that could cause serious behavioral, cognitive, emotional or mental disorders.

Extended Family — Any family members outside of your immediate family such as grandparents, aunts and uncles.

FAD — Foster/Adoptive Home Developer. The worker assigned to monitor and assist foster families.

FAE — Fetal Alcohol Effects. A condition brought on by prenatal alcohol exposure. This is a damaging condition, like FAS, affecting the fetus that can cause mental disabilities to the child.

Family Investigator — The state employee that investigates the biological family of a child to determine if abuse or neglect has occurred.

FAS — Fetal Alcohol Syndrome. A condition brought on by prenatal alcohol exposure. This is a damaging condition affecting the fetus that can cause both physical and mental disabilities to the child.

FASD — Fetal Alcohol Spectrum Disorders. A range of disorders created by prenatal alcohol exposure.

Foster/Adoptive Home — An individual home that is certified to both foster and adopt children.

Foster Care — The temporary care of a foster child by anyone other than its biological family.

Foster Child — A child who is placed in foster care.

Foster Family Home — An individual home that is certified to care for foster children with no more than six children in the home.

Foster Group Home — An individual home that is certified to care for foster children with up to 12 children living in the home.

Foster Home — An individual home that is certified to care for foster children.

Foster Parent — The certified parent assigned to care for a foster child.

Foster Placement — Placing a child in the care of a foster parent.

FPA — Foster Parent Association. An association for foster parents to offer support to each other, pass on news and information, and to receive training.

GAL — Guardian Ad Litem. A CASA worker or a person appointed by the court to advocate to the judge on behalf of the foster child.

Home Study — The process and written report for the investigation of a home to be certified as a foster or adoptive home. It contains information on all aspects of the prospective foster/adoptive parent's medical and criminal history and all other pertinent information on all adults in the home.

HSEGH — Health, Social, Educational and Genetic History. The report that shows the health, social, educational and genetic history of the child and all known biological relatives to them.

Legal Guardian — The person or people assigned as the legal caretakers of a child.

Legal Risk — Sometimes called "at risk". A term for the placement of a child who is legally free for adoption, but is not yet being placed for adoption.

Life Book — A book containing pictures and writing that describes the life of the child while in care.

Malnourished — Insufficient diet or poor nutrition that affects the person.

Medicaid — The medical insurance program provided for all children in foster care by the state government.

Medical Consenter — The person designated by the state to consent to the medical treatment of a foster child, usually one of the foster parents.

Meth Baby — The term used to describe a baby born to a mother who used methamphetamines and who may also be addicted to the drug at birth.

Minimum Standards — The rules and regulations set forth, by the states, that govern foster families.

Neglect — Lack of care and supervision of a child.

PAL — Preparation for Adult Living. A service provided for 16 to 18 year old foster children that prepares them for adult living.

Paternity Test — A DNA test to determine the biological father of a child.

Permanency Plan — The plan developed by the PPT that must be followed by all parties involved in a child's case to determine the permanency of the child.

Physical Abuse — Any physical injury or maltreatment of a child.

PMC — Permanent Managing Conservatorship. A term used to describe the care of a child who remains in the conservatorship of the state until they are 18 or have graduated from high school.

PMN — Primary Medical Needs. A foster home that cares for medically fragile children.

PPT — Permanency Planning Team. A team composed of state employees and other involved parties that evaluates and determines the course of action for a child in care.

PRIDE — Parent Resource for Information Development Education. The curriculum designed to train new foster parents and prepare them for foster care.

Private Agency — Independent privately run agency that provides foster care. A foster family may choose to work directly with DFPS or with an independent agency. The children serviced all come from the state system.

Psychotropic Medicine — Drugs that treat emotional, behavioral and mental illnesses.

RAD — Reactive Attachment Disorder. The inability of a child to attach to others generally as a result of previous relationships.

Relinquishment — Voluntarily giving up the parental rights to your biological child through the signing of a document. The actual document is often called the "Relinquishment".

Respite Care — Temporary care of the child by another family provided for the relief of a foster family.

Glossary of Terms and Acronyms

Reunification — The act of returning a foster child to the care of its biological parents.

Sexual Abuse — Causing a child to act or engage in a sexual manner with an older person.

Surrogate Parent — A person who takes the place of and acts as the parent to a child.

Termination of Rights — The process and act of removing all parental rights of a biological parent.

TFFA — Texas Foster Family Association. An organization in Texas that works to improve the well-being of children and their families, assist foster families and works to improve the foster care system. Other states may have similar organizations.

Therapeutic Home — A foster home that cares for basic and therapeutic children.

WIC — Women, Infants, and Children. A federal agency that provides nutrition information and certain foods to eligible participants.

Order Form

Order additional copies of *Foster Parenting: A Simple Guide to Understanding What It's All About* using the order form below or order online at www.starikpublishing.com

Yes, I want ____ copies of *Foster Parenting: A Simple Guide to Understanding What It's All About* for $14.95 each.

Include $3.50 shipping and handling for one book, and $1.00 for each additional book. Texas residents must include applicable sales tax.

Payment must accompany orders. All orders will be shipped via media mail.

My check or money order for $_____ is enclosed.
Please charge my ❏ Visa ❏ Mastercard

Name _____

Organization_____

Address _____

City/State/Zip _____

Phone _____

E-mail _____

Card # _____

Exp. Date _____

Signature _____

Make your check payable and return to
Starik Publishing
P.O. Box 307
Slaton, TX 79364

Or order online at
www.starikpublishing.com